D1098019

DUCK DECOYS

COLOR PATTERNS FOR DECOYS *Dr. Edgar Burke*

MALLARD (Male) MALLARD (Female)

PINTAIL (Male) PINTAIL (Female)

BLACKDUCK (Natural Cork) BLACKDUCK (Wood)

GREEN-WINGED TEAL (Male) GREEN-WINGED TEAL (Female)

DUCK DECOYS

HOW TO MAKE THEM
HOW TO PAINT THEM
HOW TO RIG THEM

By

EUGENE V. CONNETT, 3rd

Illustrated by

DR. EDGAR BURKE

AND THE AUTHOR

DURRELL PUBLICATIONS

Distributed by

The Stephen Greene Press

120 Main Street

Brattleboro, Vermont 05301

Library of Congress Catalogue Card No. 53-8764

Fourth Printing

Printed by Universal Lithographers, Inc.
Bound by L. H. Jenkins, Incorporated

DEDICATION

. . . and this one is for

BEVAN

BOOKS BY THE AUTHOR

WING SHOOTING AND ANGLING
MAGIC HOURS
FEATHERED GAME FROM A SPORTING JOURNAL
ANY LUCK?
FISHING A TROUT STREAM
RANDOM CASTS
THE SMALL BOAT SKIPPER
DUCK DECOYS

Preface

I recently was given a necktie which had little decoy ducks embroidered on it. With it came a paper slip which read: "The Decoy Duck. The hunter's most loyal friend—an effortless performer of great patience—truly a rare bird." *

An effortless performer of great patience! I never heard a more delightful description of a wildfowl decoy.

A North American Indian made the first duck decoy, maybe a thousand years ago. One of them was found in a desert cave; it was a canvasback made of reeds, and had some white feathers along its sides. There was no mistaking the species.

Since that time other Indians and many white men have fashioned decoys of all species with which to lure wildfowl within the range of their weapons. These men knew ducks and geese—their habits, their kinds, their worth. What some of them didn't know was that their seemingly untold millions could be reduced by drought and over-gunning to a dangerously low level. But we know that today, and we kill fewer of them, and we no longer toll them in with live birds. We rely on counterfeit birds, and we have learned that the more true-to-life we make these, the more effective they are, and the more pleasure we derive from their use.

So I have written down what I know about fashioning these fascinating "effortless performers of great patience" in the hope that you will discover and enjoy some of the pleasure I have had in making and using a rig of fine hand made decoys.

I think it adds some, may I say dignity, to the art of decoy

* By G. S. Harvale and Company.

making to remember its antiquity, and to think back on those skilful carvers who practiced this waterfowl portraiture before our grandfathers were born. I find that it keeps me from being satisfied with anything much less than the best I can do when shaping and painting each decoy. You must never forget that some day some one may come across one of yours and add it to his collection of old decoys. If it carries your name (which it should, on its bottom) you will rest easier if it is a fine specimen of the art of decoy making.

EUGENE V. CONNETT, 3RD.

Bellport, Long Island.
June, 1953.

Table of Contents

List of Illustrations

Dr. Edgar Burke

Goldeneye (Male)
Canvasback (Male)

Goldeneye (Female)
Canvasback (Female)

CHAPTER I

Introductory

I made my first duck decoy in 1915, a mallard to be used in the Hanover Neck swamp in New Jersey. It was hollow wood, and not many years ago I reshaped it and turned it into a pintail. This last fall I shot over it in the rig of one of my friends to whom I had given it several years ago. It may be safely said that a good duck decoy is a good investment!

The last dozen decoys I made were completed one at a time. This might not seem to be the most efficient manner in which to have done them, many makers advising that bodies and heads should be turned out in lots of half a dozen or so. As far as the setting up of any machinery is concerned, this is true; but I have found that completing a single decoy will develop small improvements in each one as you go along, to say nothing of refinements in methods. As the late Joel Barber used to insist, decoy making is a form of tidewater *sculpture,* and I doubt whether any sculptor would work in a wholesale manner. But please yourself in this matter; do it in any way that seems easiest. I should add that it is really helpful to make a number of heads at one time—in fact, all that you may require for the rig you are building. But the making of bodies, the setting of heads and the final fairing up and finishing can best be done one at a time in my opinion. No two of my decoys are exactly alike, nor would I want them to be. No live ducks are exactly alike, either.

I am extremely fortunate in being able to reproduce in this book a series of body and head patterns which originally belonged to the late Mr. John H. Boyle, famous decoy maker of Bellport, Long Island. After Mr. Boyle's death these patterns were given to my friend Mr. Theodore T. Everitt, also of Bellport, and he has been kind enough to place them in my hands so that I might trace them and make them available to all who may read this book. In addition to these I am reproducing my own black duck heads and body patterns. These patterns have been evolved over the years as a result of actual shooting experience and familiarity with hundreds of decoys which have been produced by dozens of skillful decoy makers.

It must be remembered that two different decoy makers will arrive at two different results from the same pattern; that is why each maker's decoys are so individual. But good patterns you *must* have to start with, and good patterns are very hard to come by. If this book has no other merit, the head and body patterns alone should prove of inestimable value to all decoy makers.

In addition to these features I am fortunate in owning a collection of paintings of decoys made by the late Dr. Edgar Burke, a lifelong friend and sporting companion. Many of these are being reproduced in black and white and color as a guide in painting decoys of various species. As far as I know, those shown in black and white are the only paintings which indicate the plumage patterns for decoys from both the side and top views. The text explains the correct colorings and how to mix the paints used for them. As you have the pattern of the plumage, and the instructions for mixing the colors, you are equipped to do a good job.

One word of caution: don't waste your time and efforts on poor material. A lot of time and effort is involved in making a really first class decoy, and the finished result should last for many years, under all the conditions it may meet with.

Unless you have used first class materials, you will not have invested your work wisely.

Never miss an opportunity to study the decoys of other makers; look for their faults as well as their virtues. When gunning over another man's rig, cast a critical eye on how the decoys act in rough weather—as well as smooth. Try to figure out why some don't act as they should, and why others do. You will find a good deal about this subject in the book; but nothing is more valuable than studying decoys under actual conditions of use.

In recent years there has grown up a tendency among decoy makers to give undue consideration to the appearance of a decoy in the hand, or on the mantelpiece. I deplore this tendency, although I realize that it has contributed importantly to the proper painting of decoys. The only way to judge the merits of *gunners'* decoys is to shoot over them, under all conditions. And the only way a wildfowler should design and build his decoys is with a view to what they look like *to the ducks,* and how they behave on the water, and whether they can stand the gaff of actual gunning, and whether he can transport them, set them out and pick them up under the most difficult as well as the easiest conditions the weather and his locality may provide.

The man who has shot wildfowl for many years, but has never made his own decoys, should be able to produce better decoys than the man who is an expert with tools and paint brushes, but who has had little experience in blind and boat. It is with both of these men in mind that I have written this book, and the former may appreciate parts of it more than the latter. But as long as wildfowl can be shot, there will always be a very numerous group of red blooded citizens who will be fascinated by the pursuit of them—which is as it should be. Whether the limit be twenty-five birds a day or four, these men will thrill to the sight of ducks pitching in to their own decoys; and I like to think that the majority of those who gunned before the days of bag limits or when one could legally kill twenty-five birds a day, still get their greatest pleasure and reward for suffering the hardships often involved in wildfowling from being competent in tolling the birds in to their rigs, whether they kill them, photograph them or miss them.

CHAPTER II

Why Make Your Own Decoys?

Recently I had a fine demonstration of the value of well made and carefully painted decoys. I have a dozen black duck stool which I made some years ago, and the fact that one of this set took second prize at The Sportsman's Show in New York indicates that these decoys are really good ones. I also have a dozen pressed cork commercial black ducks, and while they are good ones of their kind, they certainly don't look as lifelike as my own, swimming in various positions and with feather markings carefully painted in.

On the day I speak of the wind shifted three times, and each time I had to shift my rig. I started out with the commercial stool at the head of the rig, and the ducks that came in all dropped in at the *tail* of the rig—not the usual procedure, by the way. When the wind hauled I shifted the commercial decoys to the tail of rig, which happened to be the easiest way to make the necessary change, and several times ducks dropped in among my handmade decoys at the head of the rig.

The third shift put the handmade decoys at the tail of the rig once more, and again the ducks dropped into them instead of normally going to the head.

The foregoing experience, so fresh in my mind, was merely one of a number of demonstrations which have proved to me through the years that carefully designed and well painted decoys will attract ducks far more regularly than less carefully made stool.

That great wildfowler and incomparable decoy maker, the late "Shang" Wheeler, of Connecticut, wrote: "Two experiments were made by friends of the writer, one in which a flock of fifty poorly made associated species were used in one setting and another group of fifteen high grade cork decoys were set about seventy-five feet to one side of the others, so that birds leading up toward the two rigs had a chance to decide for themselves which group to hail to. The result was that all lone birds, pairs or trios went directly to the small bunch of good-looking decoys and the larger flocks chose the open water between the two settings, but favored the good-lookers. This friend wrote later: 'I would not have believed it, had I not seen it. I guess those cork decoys of yours must have had sex appeal.' " *

I could quote many other authorities on this question of the greater pulling power of really fine decoys—men such as the late Dr. Edgar Burke and the late Joel Barber, both of whom were intimate friends of mine for many years—but it hardly seems necessary to belabor the point. Nothing looks as much like a live duck as another live duck, but as we can't use live decoys these days, we must make our decoys to look and act as much like a live duck as we reasonably can—if we want to toll birds in to our rig instead of having them go to a fellow gunner with a better set of stool that we have. And we want our birds to come in peacefully, not nervously and ready to flare if a clumsy looking decoy acts abnormally.

I recently saw some black duck decoys with long necks and raised heads. They were excellent examples of nervous birds with their heads up, looking for trouble. I don't believe that wildfowl like to drop in with nervous birds. How much better to have the heads low, some reversed in the position of sleeping ducks. One or two decoys with necks stretched,

* From *Duck Shooting Along the Atlantic Tidewater,* edited by Eugene V. Connett, William Morrow & Co., Inc.

Dr. Edgar Burke

Blue-wing Teal (Male) Blue-wing Teal (Female)
Green-wing Teal (Male) Green-wing Teal (Female)

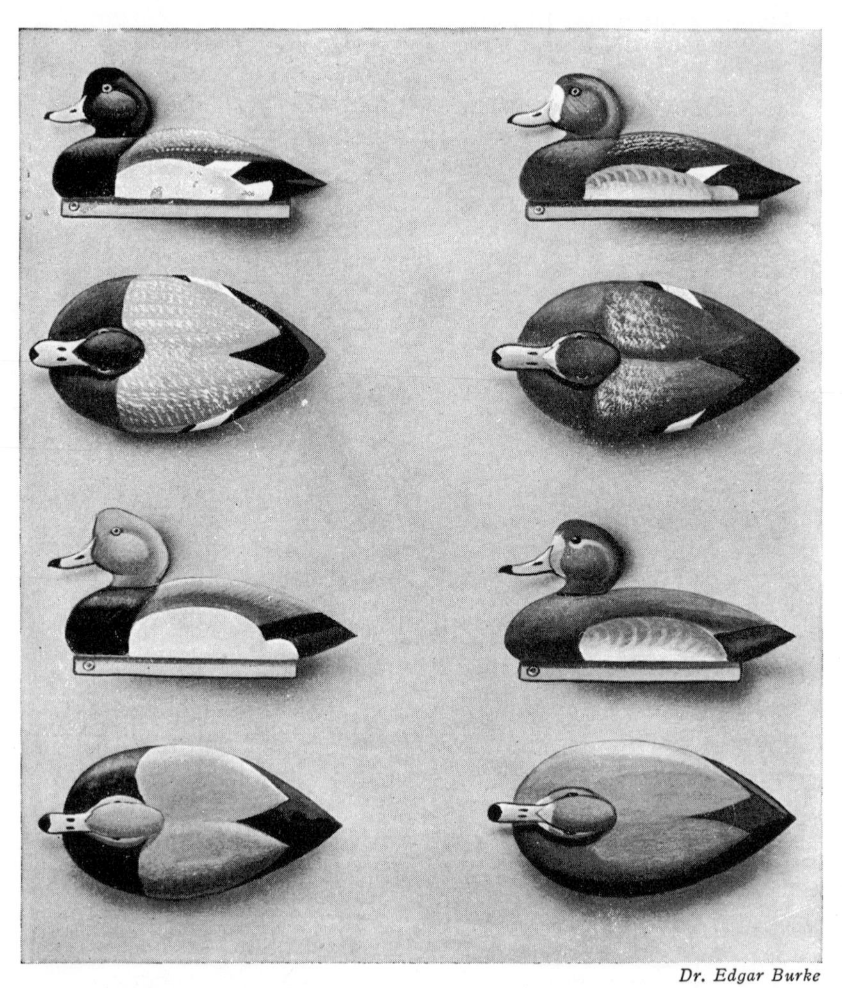

Dr. Edgar Burke

Broadbill (Male) Broadbill (Female)
Redhead (Male) Redhead (Female)

used in a rig of contented and resting birds, might give a natural effect inasmuch as a few birds will often look up—especially when calling to others on the wing.

So we must study the attitudes of live birds and attempt to design our decoys in positions which indicate that they are unworried and peaceful.

We must also construct our decoys so that they float and ride the waves like live birds. Decoys which roll from side to

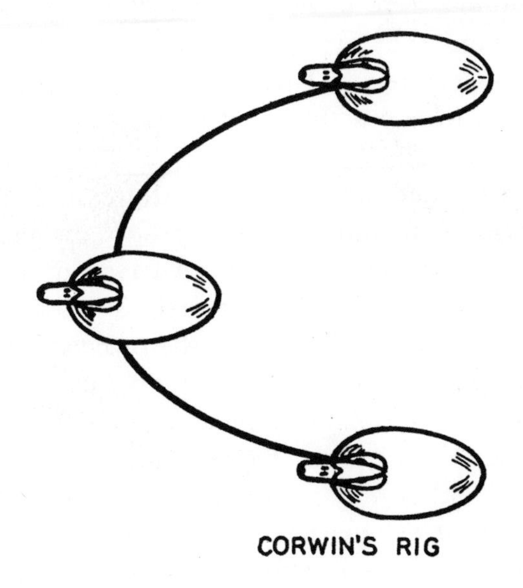

CORWIN'S RIG

side look unnatural, because live ducks don't roll; they ride breast to the waves and necessarily pitch, but don't roll. This matter will be more fully covered when we come to the actual designing and constructing of the decoys. In this connection it may be of interest to describe the manner in which Wilbur A. Corwin of Bellport, Long Island, rigged his decoys. As they did not have to be transported far during the season, being left on punties at the different points which he gunned, it was entirely practical to rig them as he did. He would bend a quarter inch galvanized rod, about four feet long, in a semicircle, and securely staple a decoy at each end and one in the middle of the rod, so that the three stool were parallel to each other. (See sketch.) Then only one anchor line was required for three decoys and they couldn't roll in the least. Each end of the rod was sharply bent up for about an inch, and this was sunk into the bottom of the decoy to prevent its shifting after two heavy galvanized staples had secured it to the rod. This is a splendid way to rig stool in circumstances where they don't have to be transported under difficult conditions. Imagine the saving in time when setting out and picking up a sizeable rig. I used this method for many years and know it to be practical and successful from first hand experience.

Where I gun there are some forty different rigs belonging to the individual members of our group, all pulled up on the shore of an island on which we have our headquarters shack. It is an education to see the various sets of decoys, each designed and painted according to the owner's ideas. For the past fifteen years I have watched the slow but sure improvement in the majority of these rigs. For one thing, we always shoot two men to a point. If one of these has a fine set of stool and the other has a nondescript, badly painted and rigged set, the latter may hear a few remarks before the day is over if the birds are not coming in well, because the two sets of decoys are rigged as one. Under such circumstances it is wise to put some of the best decoys at the head and the tail of the rig, with other good ones scattered around the edges, hoping that the birds will get their first impressions from these lifelike decoys.

To sum up: there is no doubt that in these days of relatively scarce wildfowl and very heavy gunning pressure, a set of decoys just can't be too lifelike in regard to attitude, coloring and behavior. Forty-five years ago, when I started shooting ducks, it was a different matter; if one bunch didn't come in to the rig, the next lot would and it was often easier to kill twenty-five birds then, especially if a pair of live callers was tethered in the rig, than it is to kill four today.

CHAPTER III

Decoys for Different Conditions

The decoys needed for shooting in the pin oak flats of Arkansas and those needed for the salt water tidal bays of Long Island can be quite different. In the former situation there may be a slight wind ruffle on the water, while in the latter, waves over a foot high with porridge ice in them are often in evidence on the best gunning days.

Smooth water decoys need not be as large as those used in rough water, as the former show up much better than those which are set out in the wide open sounds and bays. Often the duck call is used to draw the birds' attention to a set of stool set out in small ponds, rivers or wooded shallows. In open water, where there may be ten rigs of decoys in the sight of flying ducks, oversize stool can, and often do, prove more attractive than a smaller set, with or without calling.

Another difference in decoys involves their weight. If the gunner has to lug a set of stool through the woods and swamps, he wants them as small and light as can be and still have them effective in attracting birds. Where decoys are carried in or on a duck boat, they can be larger and heavier, and they must be sturdier in many rugged localities.

Some years ago ice scooter shooting was popular on the Great South Bay of Long Island. After the bay froze over, a scooter, painted white, with metal runners, was shoved over the surface with a sharpshod pole, to a water hole. A set of hollow wood whistler decoys, slim, light, and low, and easily stowed under the deck of the scooter, was rigged in the water hole and on the ice around its edge. One can spot a scooter decoy easily, due to its slim and low design. This type of decoy might well be used when the gunner has to carry a sack full of them any distance to a sheltered pond hole. A modern oversize mallard or canvasback would take up as much room as two of the old time scooter decoys.

Each part of the country develops a style of decoy that many long years of gunning have evolved as being best for the local conditions. Often the availability of some material in a locality will influence the kind of decoy made there. For instance, in southern New Jersey there was a plenitude of white cedar; at many saw mills one was welcome to all the odd pieces he could lug away, and the Barnegat Bay stool were usually hollow cedar. Along the south shore of Long Island an industrious beachcomber could pick up many slabs of cork from old life preservers, and Great South Bay decoys are predominantly of natural cork.

It is my intention to describe the making of various types of decoys made of several different materials, so that a gunner living almost anywhere in the country may select the design and material most favored for his locality.

In this connection it may be well to point out that a decoy anchor which is satisfactory in the Arkansas bottoms may be worthless in Long Island Sound where the tide rises and falls six feet, and the water can be exceedingly rough. In the sheltered water the anchor may be of any design, but in unprotected tidal waters it must be heavier and designed like a mushroom anchor, and much longer anchor lines are used. It is a fearful sensation to watch decoys start to drag as the tide comes up on a stormy day. When one has to launch a boat in order to retrieve dragging stool, it is not only hard work but is always a signal for birds to start coming in. However, they never get over the rig because the decoy retriever naturally scares them away.

Now, when long anchor lines are used they must be wrapped around each decoy as it is picked up, else a terrible snarl will result. In order to minimize the possibility of these wrapped lines slipping off the decoy body, it should be designed with reasonably straight sides and level back—without ruining the appearance of the decoy. A body which is well rounded from bow to stern will not hold the wrapped line as well as one with relatively straight sides. Only the

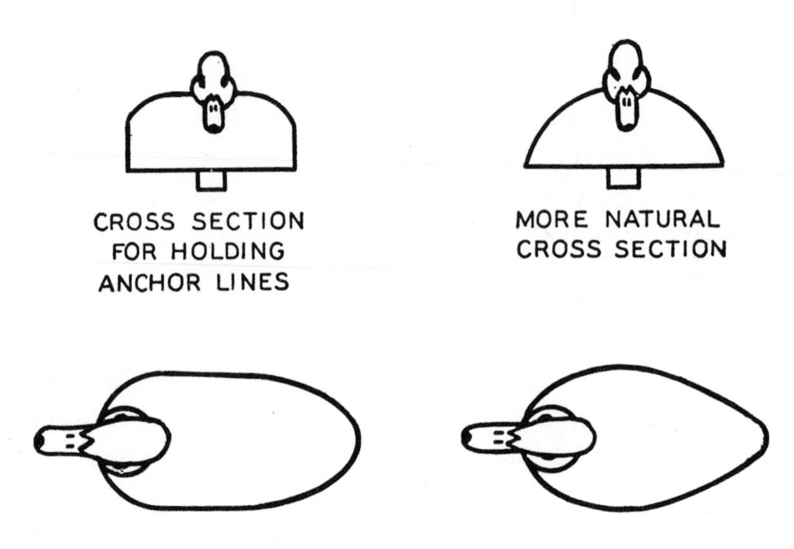

man who has had to pick up a rig of fifty ice-covered deep water stool in a living gale of wind will appreciate the importance of this.

Smooth water decoys need not be as deep as those used in rough water. The latter will show up better among the waves if they are made at least 4″ from top to bottom, while the former can be less than 3″—especially if made of balsa with no ballast weights attached.

Rough water decoys should have keels and a lead weight on the keel to prevent them from capsizing. If a decoy lands upside down when being set out, it must immediately right itself. I have often seen three links of quarter inch chain, stapled at one end so that it hangs down from the keel, used instead of a lead weight; but lines can catch in the chain, and in my opinion the loose chain will not right a capsized decoy as quickly as a stable weight. Naturally the addition of ballast tends to make the decoy float lower in the water, and this is, therefore, an additional reason for making rough water decoys deeper through the body.

Before undertaking the somewhat sizeable job of making a set of fine decoys, study the conditions under which you plan to use them. Look at fellow gunners' decoys with an eye to gaining information about the local customs. I refer, of course, to hand made decoys, as commercial decoys may be the same the country over. If you know an old time gunner, pick his brains for information on what kind of stool he favors—and why.

Lastly, decide how many decoys you will need for the type of gunning you plan to do. In a small pond, especially in the early part of the season, four to six stool will do the trick. Later on, when the flocks of migrating birds have become larger, you will need more, and probably showier decoys. For instance, in the early season when pond hole shooting, use a few hen mallards; later on add a number of bright male birds to the hens. If you are going to shoot shoal water ducks on extensive, open water, twenty-five decoys is more than enough early in the season; later on more can be used to advantage. For deep water ducks, the more the better in my experience. I have shot from a battery with three hundred broadbill stool around it, and on the Chesapeake many battery rigs contained several hundred canvasback. But the battery is a thing of the past, so you don't have to make a couple of hundred light fowl decoys. Twenty-five should be enough. I have seen Canada geese stool to two or three decoys with plenty of good calling. But on a Mississippi sand bar I would suggest that a dozen would do a better job in attracting the honkers. In a stubble field twelve to twenty decoys would not be out of line, part of them being shadows.

Shadows are silhouettes of geese, made of ½″ marine plywood. The heads and sticks on which they stand can be hinged to the body with a small bolt and wing nut. This permits the shadows to be transported easier than would be the case if the heads and sticks were fixed. Locust makes the best stick as it is almost indestructible.

Goose shadows by T. T. Everitt.

Shadows with sticks and heads folded.

E. V. Connett

Peaceful mallards with heads down.

Frank DuFresne—Fish & Wildlife Service

Peaceful pintails with heads down.

H. M. Worcester—Fish & Wildlife Service

Nervous canvasbacks with heads raised.

CHAPTER IV

Diving and Shoal Water Ducks

There is a very decided difference in the appearance of diving ducks and shoal water ducks as they sit on the water. The former "squash" down, become much broader than when in the air, and their tails slant down toward the surface. Broadbill, canvasback, redheads, whistlers, etc. are diving ducks.

The shoal water ducks—mallards, black ducks, widgeon, pintail, teal, gadwall—do not flatten out as much, and their tails slant upward. (See sketches.)

The necks of the shoal water ducks are generally longer than those of the divers, with the exception of canvasback. While shoal water duck decoys should not have *extended* necks, they can have relatively longer than those of the divers, whose heads should be snuggled down into the body, showing virtually no neck.

It is important to bear in mind that a flock of resting ducks will contain birds in many different poses. But there is one occasion on which almost every bird in a swimming flock will assume the same pose: namely, when they are nervous or fearful. Then all heads come up and look in the direction of the suspected danger. A flock of contented, peaceful and unsuspicious ducks will contain birds with heads turned to one side or the other, with heads facing the rear as they sleep with their bills under their wing, with bills dabbling in the water, etc. So we must strive to get this effect in our rig of decoys. Fortunately it is quite easy to do this, as the same design of head can be set in many different positions on the bodies of various decoys.

It is quickly evident to anyone watching a flock of feeding shoal water ducks that many of them are "standing on their heads" as they reach down to the bottom in search of food.

SHOAL WATER DUCK

DIVING DUCK

A few tip ups and feeders may well be included in a rig of shoal water ducks. These will be described later.

While most shoal water ducks will decoy to a set of black duck or mallard decoys, depending on the locality, it is wise to include a few widgeon and pintail with the other birds. At present my rig consists of twenty-five black ducks, three widgeon and three pintails. This is a very satisfactory combination, and many of my friends use about the same. Often a few Canada geese are added, set a bit off to one side. While broadbill seldom drop into this rig, they do fly over it; but if I were shooting in a locality where broadbill, canvasbacks, whistlers, redheads, etc. were plentiful and likely to trade near a point, I would either use a rig entirely of broadbill and canvasbacks, or add six or eight broadbill to my shoal water rig, set off to one side a short distance, to make them more conspicuous. (See Chapter XI.)

Sometimes a rig of black ducks or mallards are set out in shoal water, with a pair of male pintails placed together outside the rest of the rig. Pintails are about the most wary ducks there are, and their presence is thought to indicate that all is serene. In days gone by a decoy gull was sometimes used for the same purpose.

I have never found that it did any harm to use normal and oversize decoys together. In fact, I believe that it is a good plan, as there are larger and smaller live birds in a flock. In other words, a rig that is varied in the attitude and size of the individual decoys, looks more natural than a rig of decoys all in one position and all exactly the same size. Anything that tends to make your decoys look more like a flock of happy, live birds is worth striving for.

CHAPTER V

Materials

The best decoy making materials vary according to the conditions under which the decoys are to be used. Where light weight is a requirement, solid cork or pressed cork are excellent, as is balsa wood. However, where rough treatment is to be expected, solid cork will be the best of these three materials. I used a set of pressed cork decoys for a number of years under rugged conditions, and they finally began to disintegrate. At the same time several sets of solid cork decoys belonging to friends have stood up satisfactorily for fifteen years or more, and some balsa wood decoys seemed to stand the gaff quite well. The life of the pressed cork decoys can be materially lengthened if they are given a sufficient number of coats of paint to close all the surface interstices of the material. This can be satisfactorily accomplished with dead flat paints, and enough coats to produce a fairly smooth protective surface.

If weight is less important, white pine or cedar, either solid or hollow, will produce a very sturdy decoy which will withstand years of rough treatment. It is not always easy to find clear wood of good quality in size 4″ x 8″, which will be required for the larger species, and if hollow decoys are to be made, *clear* 2″ x 8″ wood is desirable. It took me several months to find enough good clear 2″ x 8″ white pine to make a dozen large hollow black ducks. I visited a number of lumber yards and woodworking mills before I was able to assemble my material.

Regardless of the kind of body material one chooses, there

is but one really satisfactory material for making the heads, and that is straight grain, clear white pine. White wood can also be used, as can cedar which is better; but white pine is the easiest to work and over the years has proven its worth as to strength and workability. It should be two inches thick in order to allow for carving real character into the heads. The lower cheeks must bulge and the necks must not be spindly. It is remarkable the extent to which really fine heads will put life into a set of decoys, even when the bodies are not too skillfully designed. Only when a good head splits or breaks will you fully realize the importance of using nothing but the finest well seasoned wood you can get.

It is not easy to find satisfactory natural cork these days, but there are concerns which deal in cork and if you want a set of solid cork decoys badly enough you will undoubtedly be able to obtain the required material. Two layers of two inch thick cork will produce satisfactory bodies for any species of duck, although geese will require three layers. One very nice thing about solid cork for black ducks is that it does not require painting. The most beautiful, soft finish can be achieved by burning the surface of the cork with a blow torch; it is dull and feathery looking and lasts for some years. When too much natural cork color begins to show through, give it a going over with the blow torch.

Pressed cork may be had from dealers in insulating materials. Two layers of two inch will suffice for most ducks, and two layers of three inch thick will do for geese, unless very showy goose stool are wanted; in which event three layers of three inch will produce stool that can be seen for miles. But don't forget that you will have to transport these mammoth decoys. As the bottom of all pressed cork stool consists of either ½″ pine or ⅜″ marine ply wood, this adds something to the height of the decoy body.

Other necessary materials consist of a supply of ⅜″ hard

wood dowels for fastening on heads, pinning pressed cork slabs together, or in some instances reinforcing overhanging tails on pressed cork bodies. Keels can be made of good, straight grained 7/8" x 1 1/2" pine; and these are screwed to the bottom board with either hot dipped galvanized or brass screws. Everdure screws are best when the decoys are to be used in salt water. Don't forget that you will be putting in a good many hours of careful work in making your set of decoys, and you won't be a bit happy if they start to fall apart after several seasons of gunning. I repeat that the best materials are none too good for a set of fine handmade decoys.

Regardless of what body material you may use, you will need some waterproof glue. Casein glues seem to be about as good as any for fastening bottom boards to pressed cork bodies, and for helping to hold the layers of cork together. Let the mixed glue stand for about an hour before using it. Glue will also be required in putting on heads and for doweling bodies and heads. I have used Kuhl's Seam Cement in making built-up hollow wood decoys, relying on plenty of brass screws to hold the layers tightly together. But let me point out that these decoys must not be stored in a very dry place, as the wood will tend to shrink; in one instance, the wood checked from undue dryness during the hot summer months. As wooden boat hulls are subjected to just these shrinking and swelling effects, seam cement, while it does not have the adhesive qualities of casein glue, does tend to allow for a certain amount of shrinking and swelling in the seams of the built up hollow decoy. But I prefer the glue. I have made hollow decoys with a layer of wool cloth soaked in white lead laid between the wood sections to provide watertight seams.

The materials required for painting decoys will be covered in the chapter on painting. Several grades of sandpaper, or better yet garnet paper will be required for smoothing up heads and bodies.

Glass eyes are obtainable from taxidermists. Broadbill, whistlers, and redheads have yellow eyes. Canvasback have reddish eyes. Mallards, black ducks, widgeon, teal and pintails have brown eyes. If the latter are not obtainable, black eyes will suffice, and are all right for brant and geese. However, any competent taxidermist will be able to furnish exactly the correct color and size of eye for any species in which you are interested. You might just as well have this detail right. But don't fail to use glass eyes as they provide a much more lifelike appearance than do the tacks or painted eyes sometimes seen on cheap or poorly made decoys.

Calm water decoys need not have keels, and the best way to provide a fastening for the anchor rope is to nail a rawhide loop to the bottom board with not less than three copper nails. Rawhide should be 3/8″ wide and 4½″ long for each loop; this will allow an opening of an inch, and 1¼″ for nailing when doubled over. When keels are used anchor lines are attached through a hole in the forward end of the keel.

CHAPTER VI

Patterns for Bodies and Heads

Right at the start let me say that a good decoy must have a flat bottom. In the hand, round bottom and deadrise decoy bodies may look beautiful, but out on the water they simply will not act right, rolling around in a most unnatural manner. The best way to prevent rolling is to provide a good wide flat bottom with a "hard bilge"—as the boat builders have it. Stability is essential, and a deep, narrow, rounded underbody just won't have proper stability, no matter how much weight you hang on it—and there is a very decided limit to the weight of the outside ballast that can be profitably employed. Too much ballast will sink the decoy too deep in the water and destroy a lot of the visibility that we always must strive for.

Fortunately this very necessity for a flat bottom, provides us with an excellent starting point in designing our decoy, as it gives us a base on which to build. Regardless of what body material we intend to use, we start with a flat bottom pattern, and this pattern varies somewhat in shape according to whether the decoy is a shoal water species or a diver. It also varies in size according to species, and whether we are making normal or oversize decoys.

I use clear 3/8" white pine for my patterns, and once a good pattern is produced I guard it carefully, because a lot of experimenting and imagination and hard work has gone into arriving at it. It may be of interest to tell how I made my present black duck body and head patterns. "Shang" Wheeler once

Dr. Edgar Burke

Black Duck (Cork) Black Duck (Wood)
Mallard (Male) Mallard (Female)

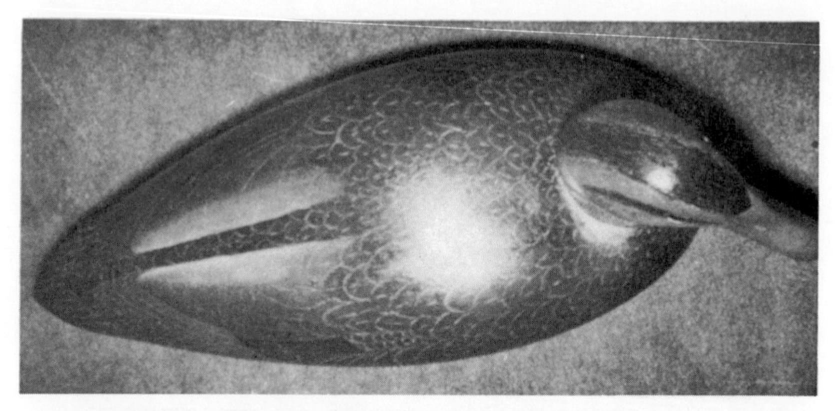

Top view of Wheeler black duck.

Three of the author's black ducks, showing various head positions.

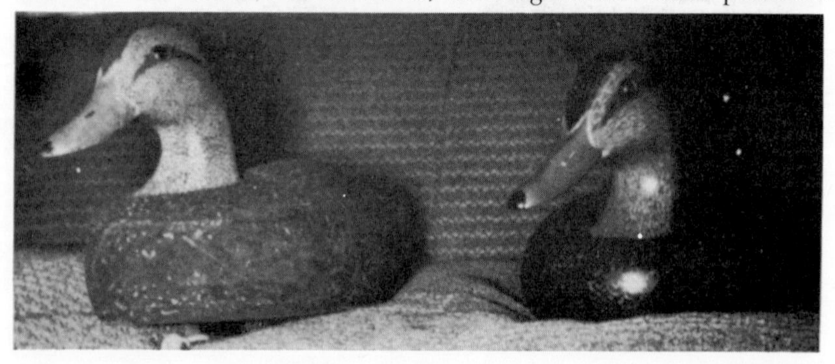

Author's black duck at left; Wheeler's at right. Note gain in stability in former.

gave me a magnificent oversize black duck decoy, avowedly made as a "mantelpiece" decoy. But it looked so much like a living black duck that I almost expected to see it flare up and fly away. However, mantelpiece decoys have no place in my gunning rig, and I had to translate this beautiful specimen into a thoroughly practical, stable, durable and lifelike decoy.

On a white panel on the bottom of this decoy, Shang had written:

To Eugene V. Connett
With my compliments.

It's wide and flat as Doctor Burke would like it,
with a life like pose as Lynn Hunt would like it,
painted something like a Black Duck as I would like it
and a bit oversize so you will like it.

I HOPE YOU DO
"Shang"

Believe me, I did like it! But for my purposes the tail was too sharp and delicate, as my decoys are carried standing on their tails in a stool rack on the after deck of my punty, and their tails must be sturdy enough to stand the wear and tear involved. Also I wanted a slightly deeper decoy that would show up better after the necessary ballast had been added. And I wanted a "harder bilge" for better stability, instead of the beautifully curved-in-at-the-bottom lines of Shang's masterpiece. While the overall length of his model measured 16½″ from tip of tail to front of breast, against my overall length of 15″, the flat bottom of his decoy measured only a scant 11″ against 12″ on mine. At the widest point his body measured 6¾″ across, against 6¾″ on mine, while the width of his flat bottom was only 5½″ against my 6½″. So you can see how I was gaining in stability without losing anything in appearance *on the water*.

In drawing the outline for my body pattern I made it 15″

long by 6¾″ wide. Being a shoal water duck, I cut away the underbody at the stern to give the necessary perked-up appearance to the tail.

You must bear in mind that the body pattern is not the same shape or size as the finished bottom of the decoy. It takes in *the extreme dimensions of the largest parts of the*

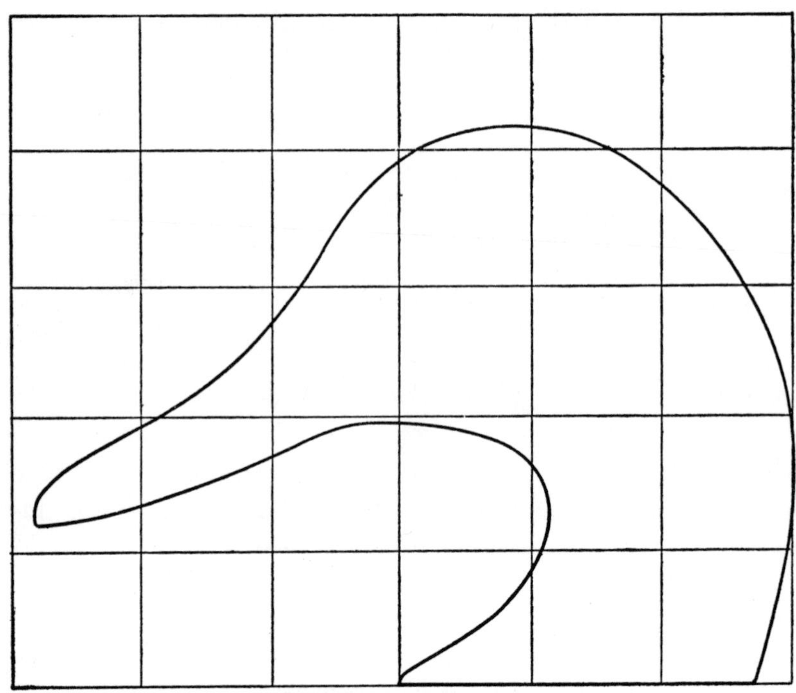

THE CONNETT BLACK DUCK

body. For instance, on shoal water ducks the under part of the tail end will be cut away, but the edges of the tail feathers on top will be approximately the size and shape of the after end of the body pattern. In other words, the pattern simply outlines the entire piece of wood or other material from which we fashion the finished body.

My two head patterns were designed from living ducks

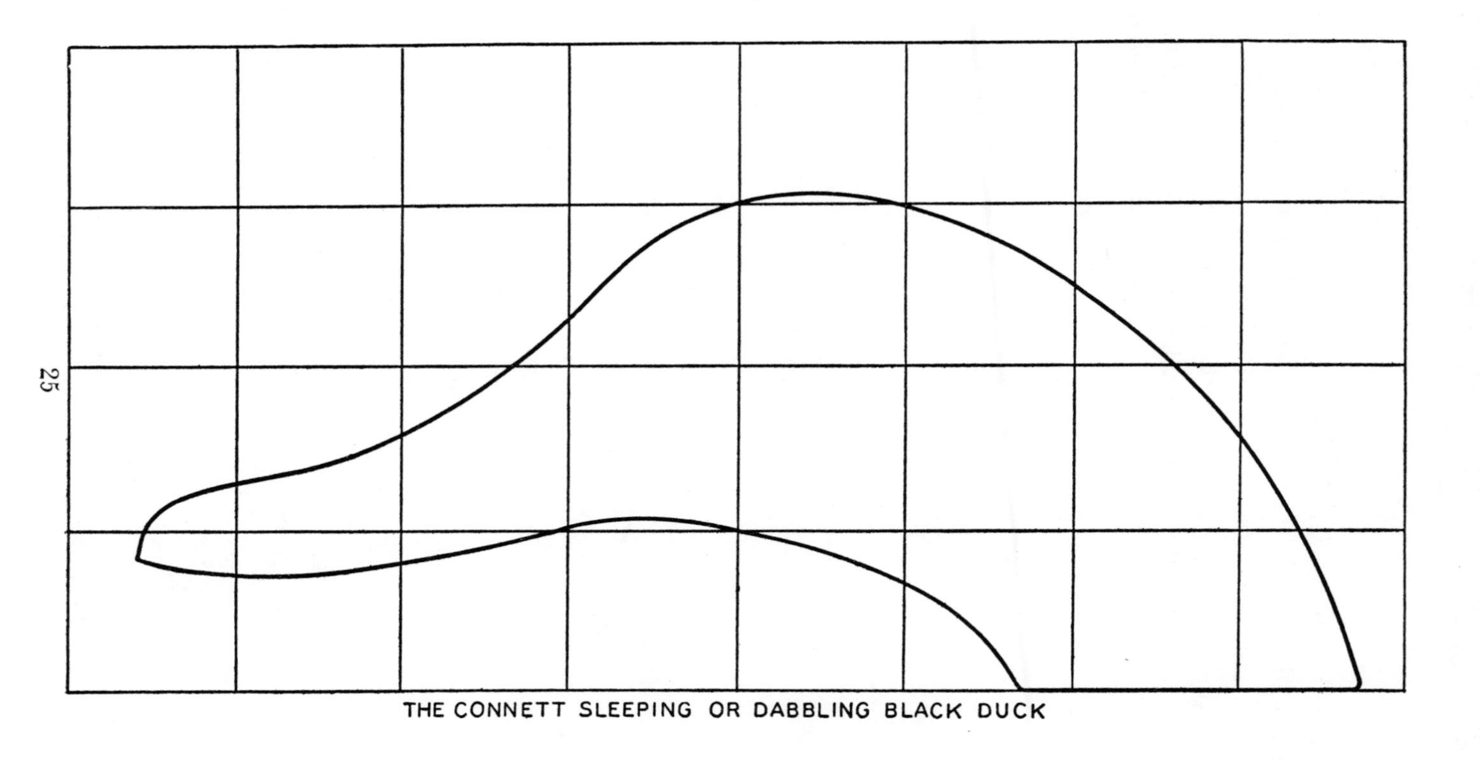

THE CONNETT SLEEPING OR DABBLING BLACK DUCK

which I watched by the hour on a lake in our local park. I also had an old head from one of Wilbur Corwin's black ducks, and of course Shang's head on the decoy he gave me. But the making of head patterns and the shaping of the heads is dependent on the knowledge of ducks, the individual skill and artistry of the maker, and a bit of luck thrown in

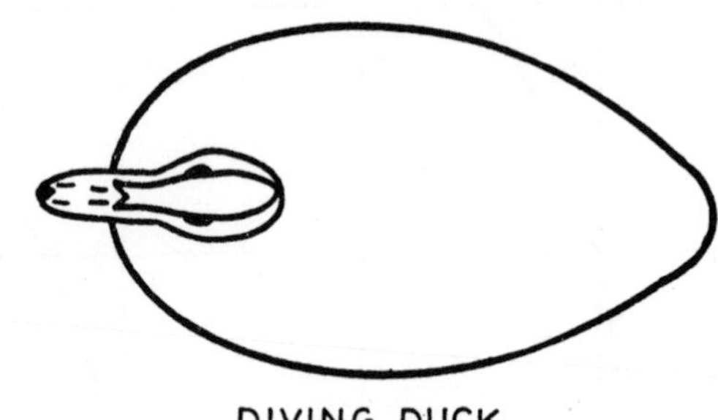

DIVING DUCK

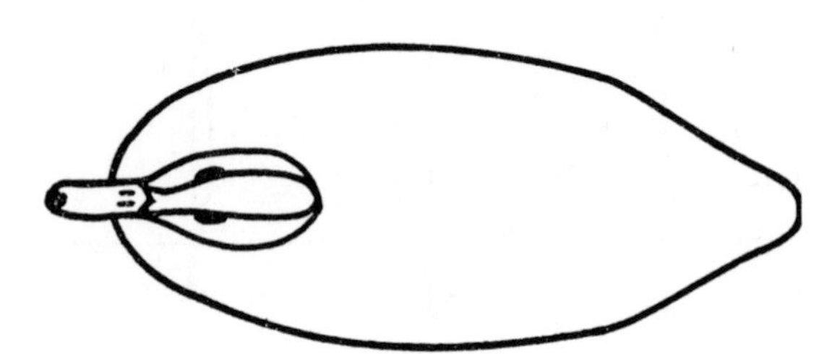

SHOAL WATER DUCK

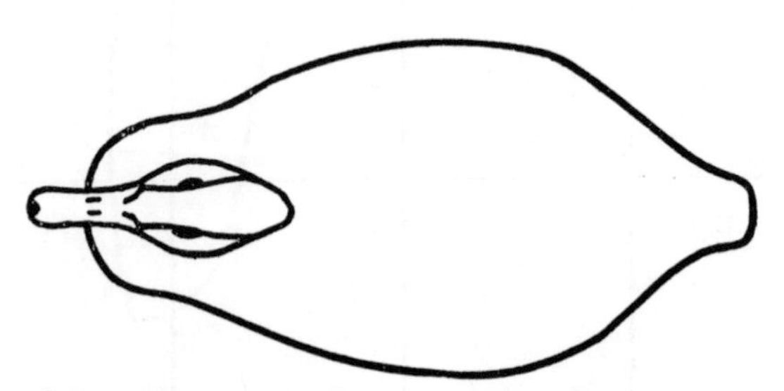

DR. BURKE'S SHOAL WATER DUCK.

for good measure. Nevertheless, a head pattern is absolutely necessary in sawing out the head in the rough. The shaping from there on is what separates the men from the boys—and incidentally makes the job so fascinating.

My lifelong friend, the late Dr. Edgar Burke, was an artist in making decoys as well as painting wildfowl on canvas. His body pattern for mallards and black ducks varied somewhat from mine, in that the body was narrower at the breast, and bulged out considerably for the middle half of the body. Reference to the sketches of my pattern and his will make this clear. It must be born in mind that Dr. Burke made bodies only of pressed cork, while I use chiefly hollow wood at the present time.

While a duck's breast is narrower than his body amidships, we must be careful about reducing the forward end of the body too much. Here is the point at which the greatest buoyancy is needed, not only because of the weight of the head, but because the anchor line is attached here and the pull of the body against the anchor tends to sink the front of the decoy. In freezing weather ice forms on the bill of the decoy and adds further weight to the forward end. I am inclined to think that Dr. Burke, in his efforts to make a decoy look as lifelike as possible, reduced the breast section of many of his decoys too much, but he shot in the South where ice was no problem.

The pattern for black duck and mallard should measure 15″ by 7″. Teal should be 11½″ long by 5½″ wide overall. Pintail should be roughly 15″ long by 6½″ wide, and widgeon 12″ long by 6½″ wide. These widths may seem a bit more than normal, but if they are made narrower the decoys will not ride well. And a resting, contented duck will flatten out quite a lot on the water. The pintail is a narrow looking duck and while it could be made a bit wider I believe it would tend to spoil the characteristic effect of the bird. The overall

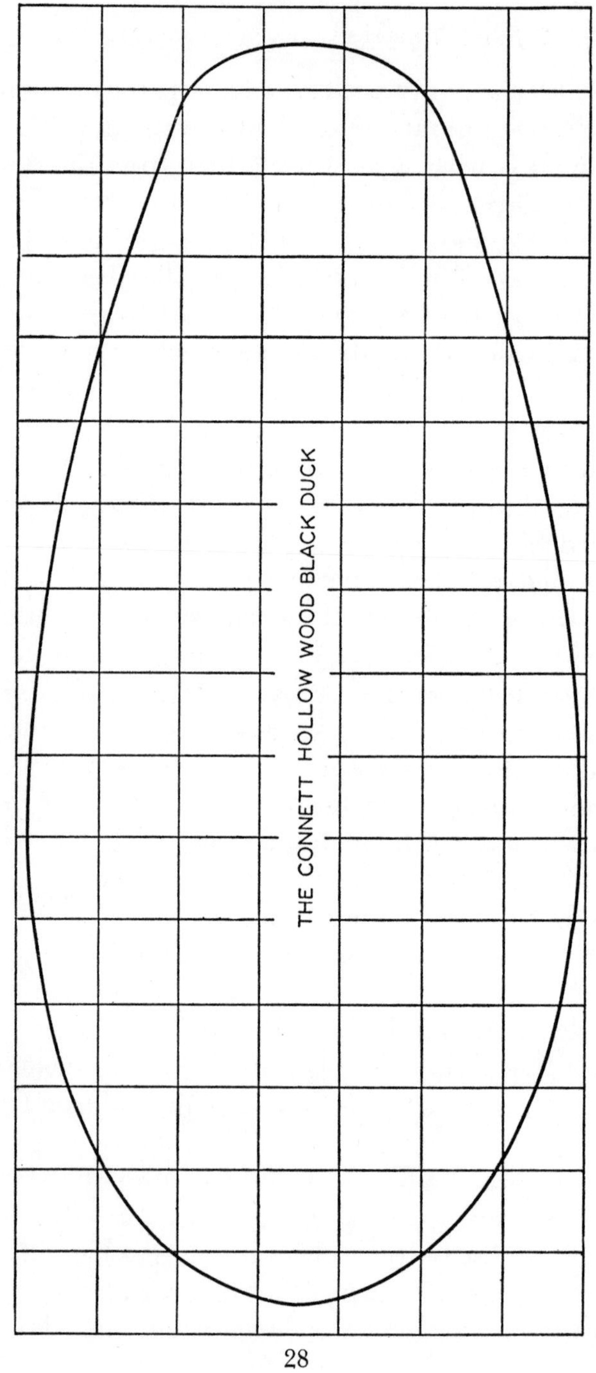
THE CONNETT HOLLOW WOOD BLACK DUCK

shape of the pattern can be about the same for all the shoal water ducks, the pintail being cut away around the tail somewhat more than the other species, to give the effect of the long tail of this species.

The head patterns for black duck, mallard and gadwall may all be the same. The pintail pattern is not so full, to give a thinner appearance, and the neck should be a bit longer to help the effect. The widgeon has a smaller bill than the mallard, as does the teal. While the black duck bill tapers very little in width, the widgeon and teal taper considerably. I urge you to study examples of good decoys in various species, and to examine any birds you kill with the greatest attention (or stuffed birds in a museum) to help you in working out your finished heads.

The pattern for broadbill decoys should be 12″ by 6½″ at the widest point. Remember that deep water fowl when resting peacefully on the water squash down and spread out more than the shoal water species do. There are two kinds of broadbill, the greater and lesser scaups. The dimensions given should do for both nicely.

The canvasback pattern should measure 15″ by 7½″. This bird is about the same size as a mallard in length, but our decoys could be wider than those for the mallard. And as the tail will slope down toward the water, instead of being high on top and cut away underneath, the dimensions I give will make a big enough decoy in the water.

Redheads will stool to broadbill (or for that matter to almost anything else, being a rather dumb duck) and I see no need for counterfeiting them. If you have the misfortune to live and shoot in a locality where you are dependent on whistlers, old squaws or coots, my best advice is to gun in some more favored clime! In my experience these birds will fly over a rig of any kind and stool to almost no rig except broadbill. Therefore, I don't suggest that you make a rig of any of these species. Please remember, this book is supposed to help the gunner make decoys over which he can shoot wildfowl. It is not aimed at telling you how to make single specimens of mantel-piece decoys to be used for door stops, cigarette boxes or spurious antiques. "Light fowl," meaning the diver species, only require broadbill and canvasback decoys from the gunner's point of view. A few whistlers for late season deep water or ice hole shooting can be added, if your locality demands.

Now we come to the king of waterfowl—the goose. I know of no greater thrill than bagging a Canada goose. I have never shot blue or snow geese, but I am reliably informed that a whisp of newspaper and a falsetto voice will bring these in. Snow geese at this time are on the restricted list, and would (and have, to my personal knowledge) decoyed nicely to a rig of black duck with a few Canada geese mixed in. I will therefore restrict my comments on patterns to the Canada goose.

On the prairies, or the sand bars of the Mississippi and the Missouri, "shadows" are effective. On salt water I have never happened to see a Canada goose lured in with them, although they work well on Currituck and Pamlico Sounds. Shadows are silhouettes about half an inch thick stuck up either in the water or on the shore. They are outlines which must be pointed in various directions so that the incoming birds get the impression that they are looking at the real thing. It is quite amusing to see the confusion in the birds' minds when some of these decoys suddenly disappear as the birds fly over them, and others appear as the birds swing around. There is no doubt that these decoys are extremely effective in stubble fields and on sand bars, but the full bodied goose decoy is best for point shooting on open tidal water of any depth.

The body pattern of the Canada goose should be 22½″ long by 9″ wide. The tail should show decided tip up, as the undertail patch of pure white is a distinctive marking, as it is in the case of the brant. In view of the very short season and low bag limit on brant, I am not suggesting that brant decoys be made. (I have shot many brant over a rig of duck stool.)

The patterns for the heads of Canada geese may include several positions: erect, or stretched out in front, as when

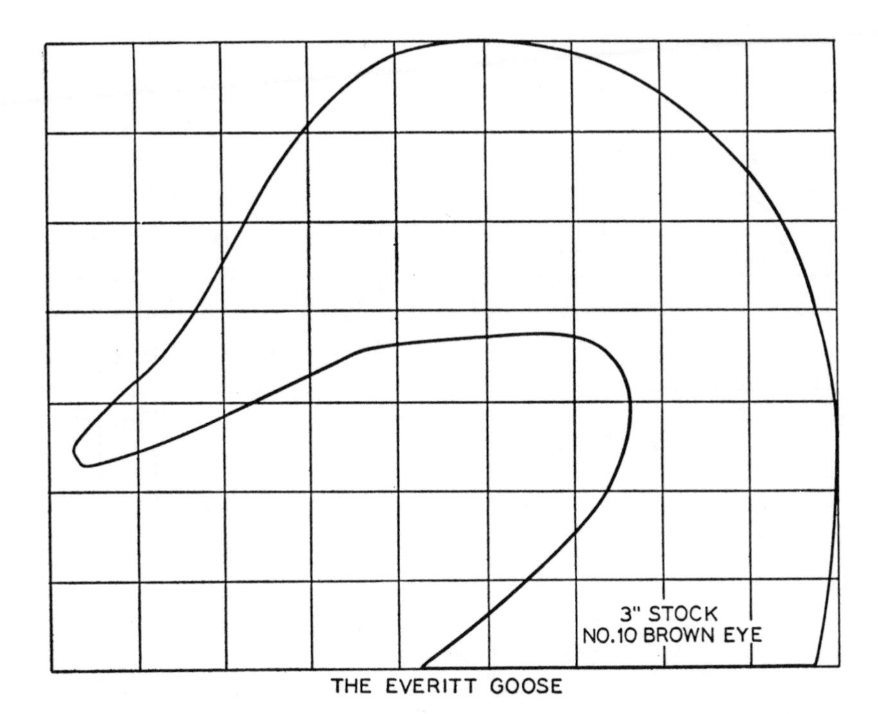

THE EVERITT GOOSE

feeding. They need not be turned from side to side as in duck decoys. As a matter of fact, when geese are tired from a long flight, they will decoy fairly readily. When they are not tired, an old gander will seldom permit his flock to decoy directly, but will let them settle on the water several gunshots beyond the stool, and then if everything satisfies him, he will slowly swim in to the decoys. First class calling will help as much as first class decoys in attracting geese. It has been my observation on the south shore of Long Island that one's best chance for a shot at a goose is when one or two young and very tired geese peel off from the flock and drop down to a

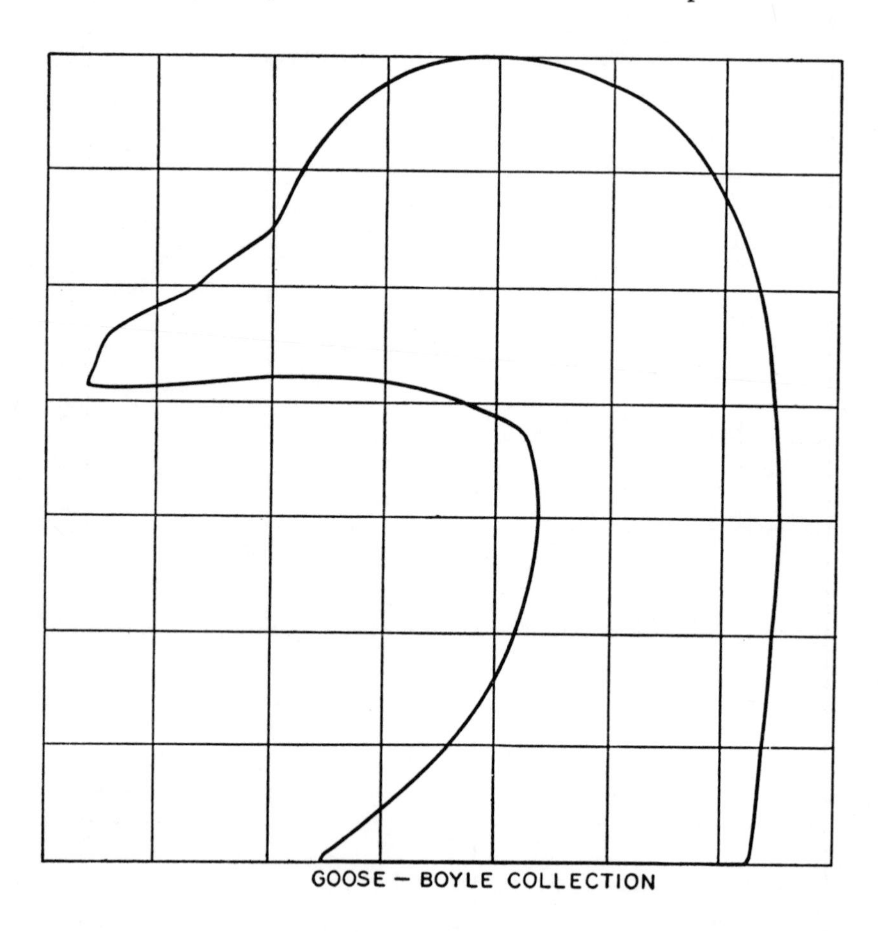

GOOSE — BOYLE COLLECTION

duck rig with a handful of goose decoys on one side. Good calling helps to tempt these young ones away from the main flock. Incidentally, the only goose fit to eat, in my humble and dentured opinion, are the young ones. An old gander is beyond the feeble efforts of what are left of my teeth.

The following section of this book, showing actual tracings of a unique collection of head and body patterns—most of them life size—can be of inestimable value to the amateur decoy maker if he thoroughly understands what they are and how to use them. All the patterns have one inch squares over them so that you may easily reproduce them in correct sizes.

First let us consider the head patterns. Some of them may appear very clumsy to the uninitiated eye, but you must always bear in mind that the pattern merely gives you the outline for sawing out the head blank. How you round out and finish this blank is what counts. But you cannot put character in a head unless there is character in the blank. Compare the Watkins black duck with the Bartow black duck; both will produce excellent heads if skillfully finished out. Watkins obviously believed in emphasizing the head of his decoy—a very desirable thing to do in many cases. Bartow was trying to make his decoy a truer copy of a live duck—also a very desirable thing to do under other circumstances. A finished head from the Watkins pattern need not look in the least clumsy and can have a most lifelike appearance when mounted on a good body and *viewed on the water.* It would "carry" well in rough water; the birds could see it and get a good impression of it at quite a distance. For smooth water the Bartow pattern would be splendid, and it would be fine for smallish bodies where transportation was a problem.

So you must study these patterns with an eye to what they will look like when finished out, and to the ultimate purpose of the completed decoy. The best way to see how the finished head will look is to make a set of heads from the patterns that interest you. Better yet make several heads from one or more patterns—you will always have use for extra heads. You will find that two heads from the same pattern can be quite different, according to how you finish them out. And if you have the necessary skill and knowledge to finish out heads with

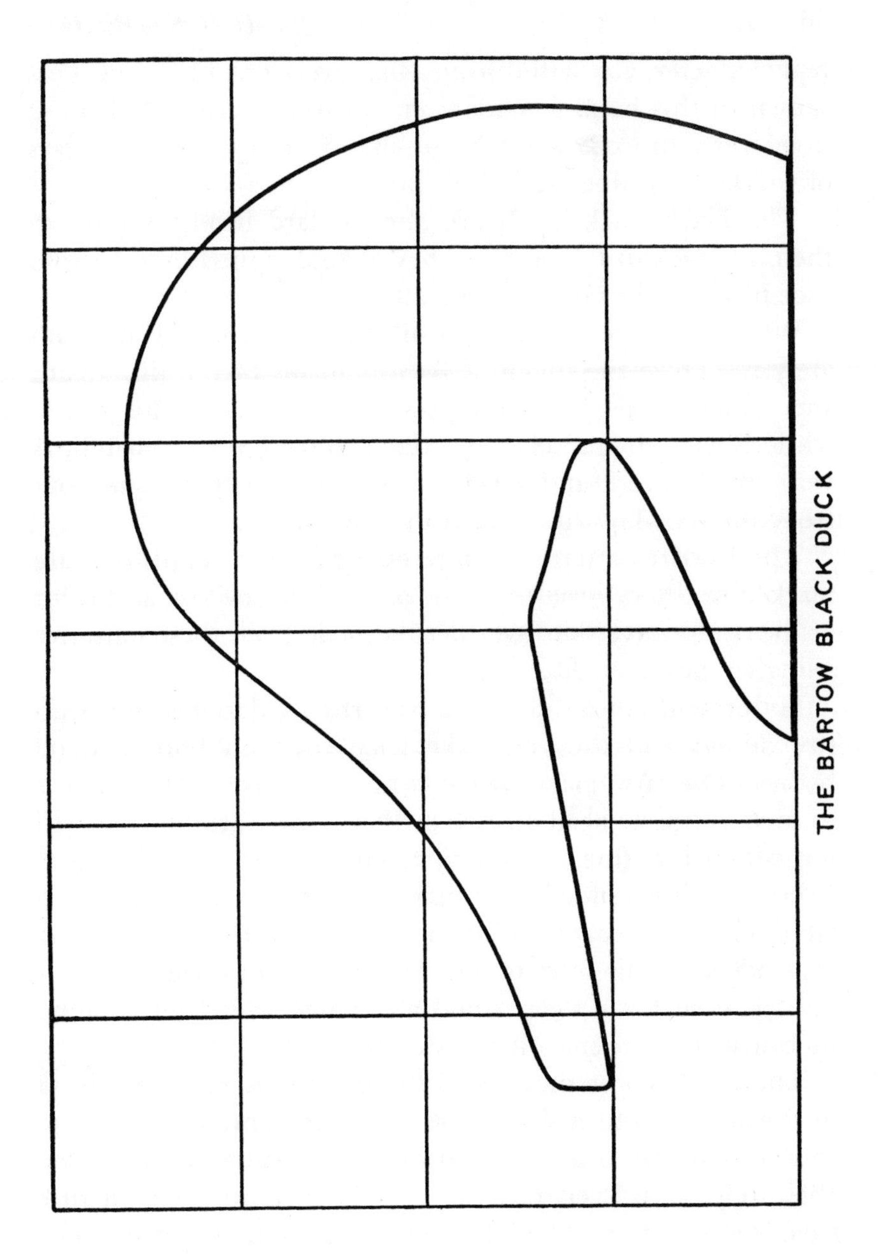

THE BARTOW BLACK DUCK

real character, you will discover that every one of the patterns shown in this book is a good one, proven by time and based upon years of experience in the use of decoys, from the days of market gunning up to the present.

The black duck heads are also mallard heads; I refer to them as black ducks because they were designed by men who shot black ducks rather than mallards.

When we come to the broadbill patterns, you will immediately recognize the touch of Bartow in his broadbill. He cut very close to his final bill profile when making his block, while Boyle left himself more wood to work on in his bill. A very sturdy head, and a very good one, can be finished out from the "Unknown" broadbill pattern.

The Everitt patterns are interesting for the details that are marked on them—the top view of the bill, the size and color of the eye. I have shot over decoys made from these patterns, and they are very effective.

My present black duck head patterns are designed for oversize decoys and thus far have been used on hollow wood bodies. The customary way in which to make a "sleeper" is to turn a regular head around so that it faces aft, but this will not produce as fine a result as making a special head such as I show. This extended head makes a very effective "dabbler," especially when turned a bit to one side. In the photo facing page 90 showing four of my decoys you can see how this head is used for a sleeper and a dabbler, the latter dipping its bill in the water as it rides each wave.

The Boyle goose measures 7″ from the crown of the head to the base of the neck; it could not be reproduced lifesize in this book. It is a beautiful head, and suitable for a sizeable body. The Everitt goose is also a very fine one which I have seen in action. The other geese all have their good points, and can be finished out with more character than you might suspect from a glance at the patterns.

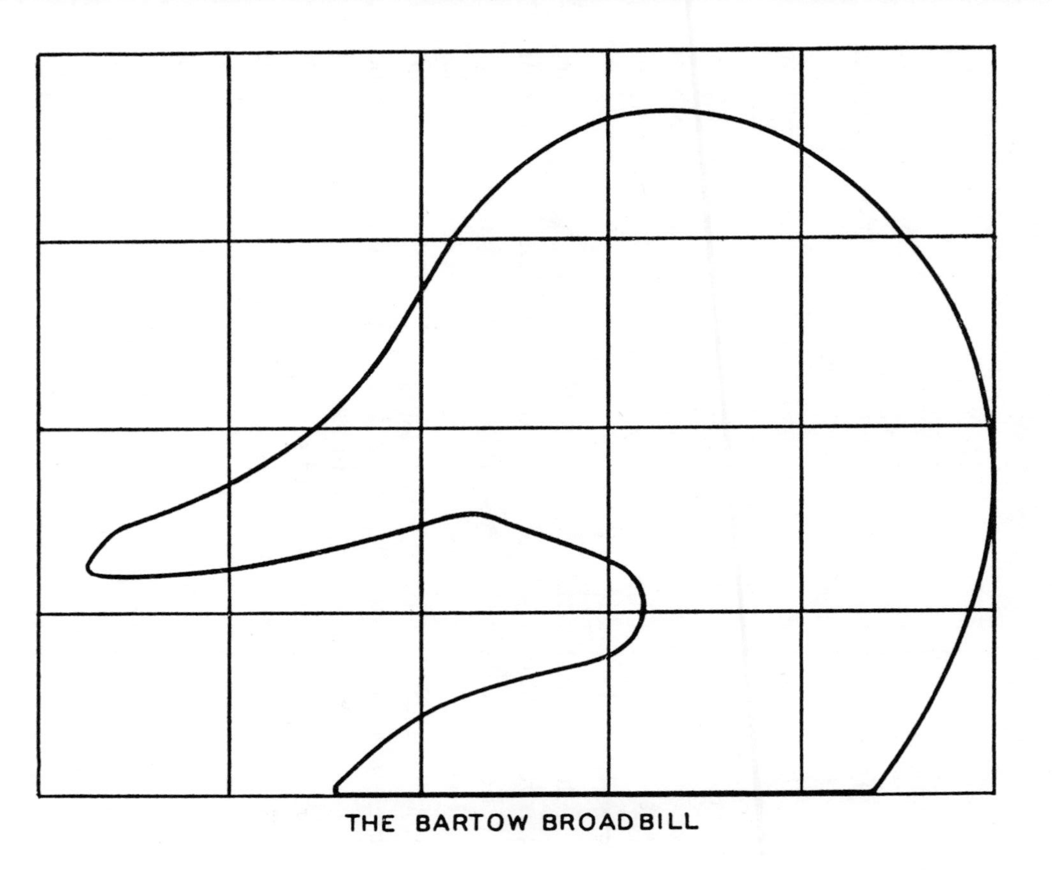

THE BARTOW BROADBILL

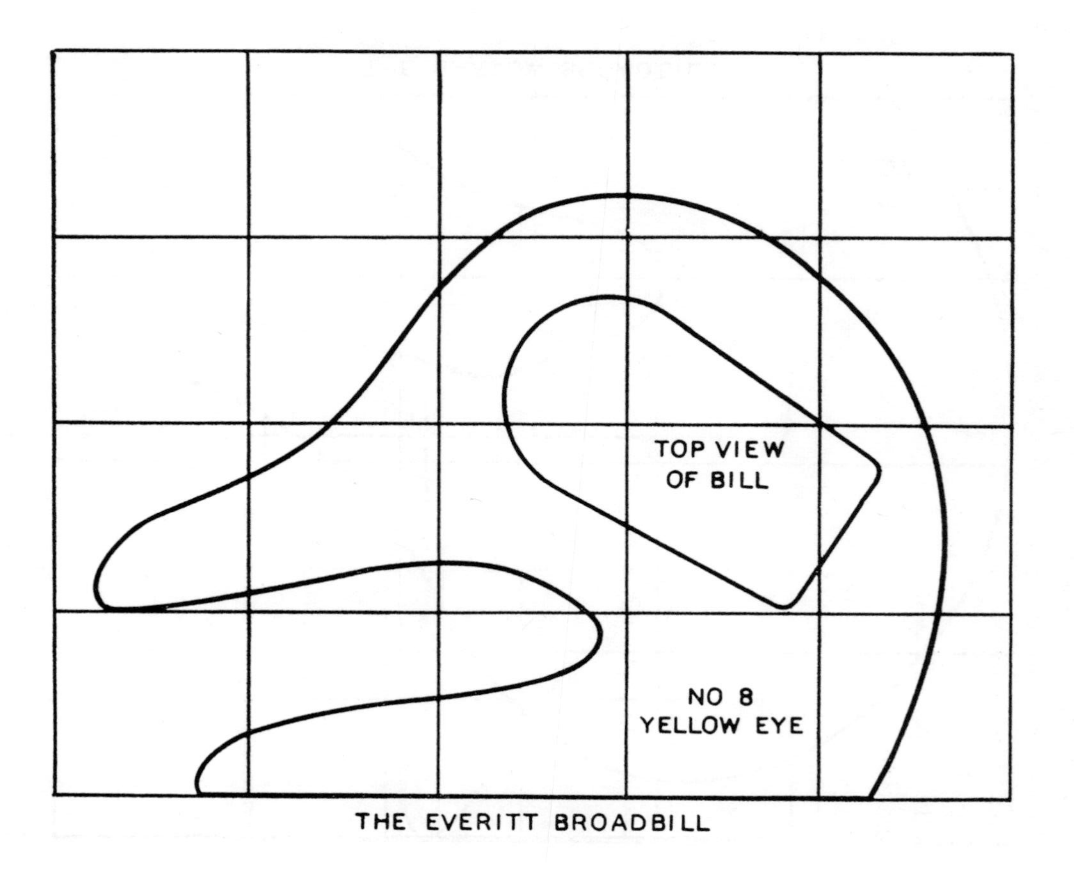

THE EVERITT BROADBILL

As body patterns are too big to reproduce lifesize in a book, I have only shown a few distinctive and representative samples. The G. Brown black duck (or mallard) body is interesting. The dotted line indicates the manner in which the under side of the tail is cut away. It will make a very stable and good looking cork body—either natural or pressed cork, but in

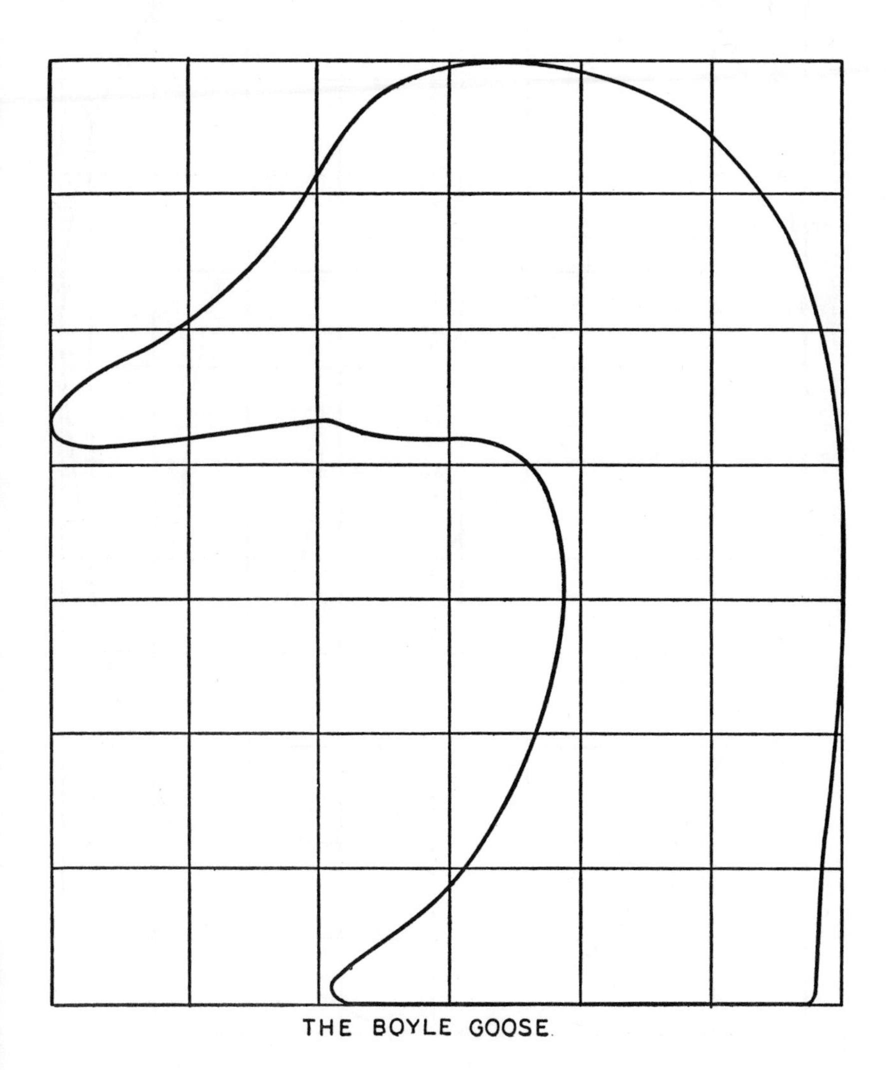

THE BOYLE GOOSE

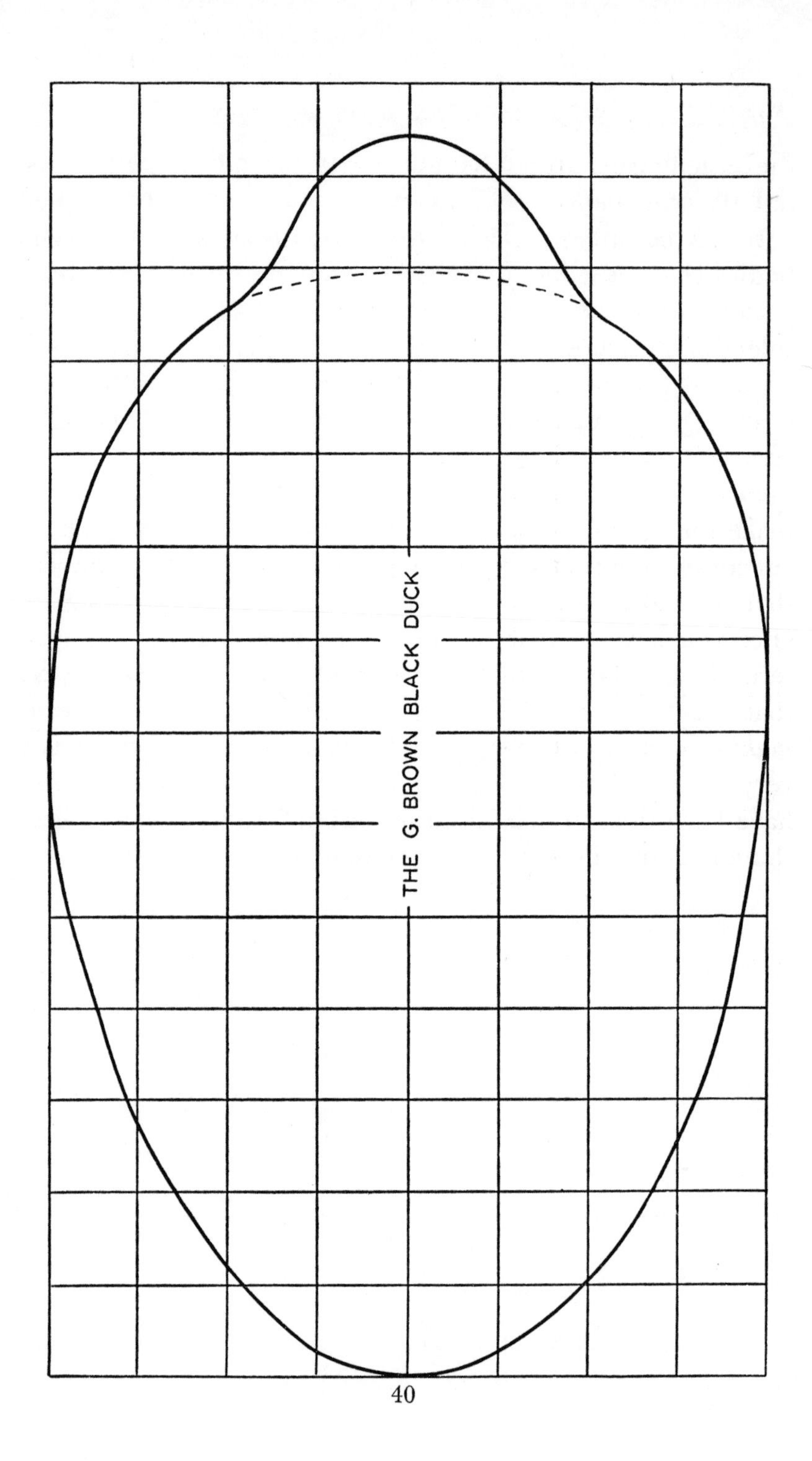
THE G. BROWN BLACK DUCK

the latter case a strengthening dowel should be used in the tail as explained elsewhere.

It may be interesting to note the variations in hollow wood bodies that have been produced from my black duck body pattern, as shown in the photograph on page 90. This is a splendid example of how the same pattern, whether head or body, can be used as the basis for decoys of individual character. For instance, the G. Brown black duck body pattern will make a fine broadbill body if reduced in size. The *plan* is splendid for a broadbill, and the correct *elevation* will make the difference—tail slanted down instead of up and not cut away underneath as for a black duck. I must point out that the more you know about decoys, and the more experience you have in making them, the more valuable the patterns in this book will become. And I want to remind you that every pattern in the book is the result of *years of decoy making and gunning experience.* In other words, there is a very sound reason for every line in these patterns, and they have been used in making hundreds of decoys, that have had thousands of wildfowl shot over them.

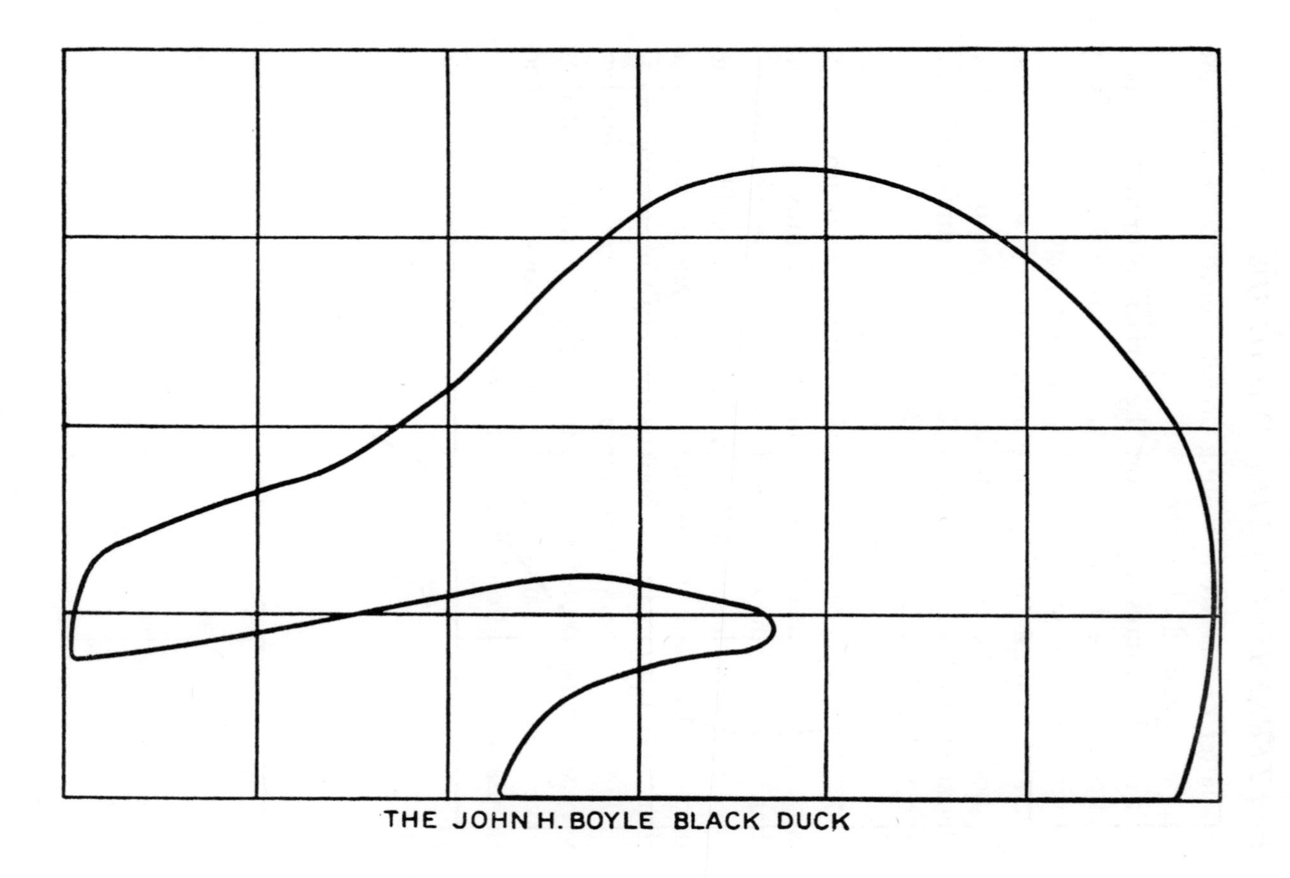

THE JOHN H. BOYLE BLACK DUCK

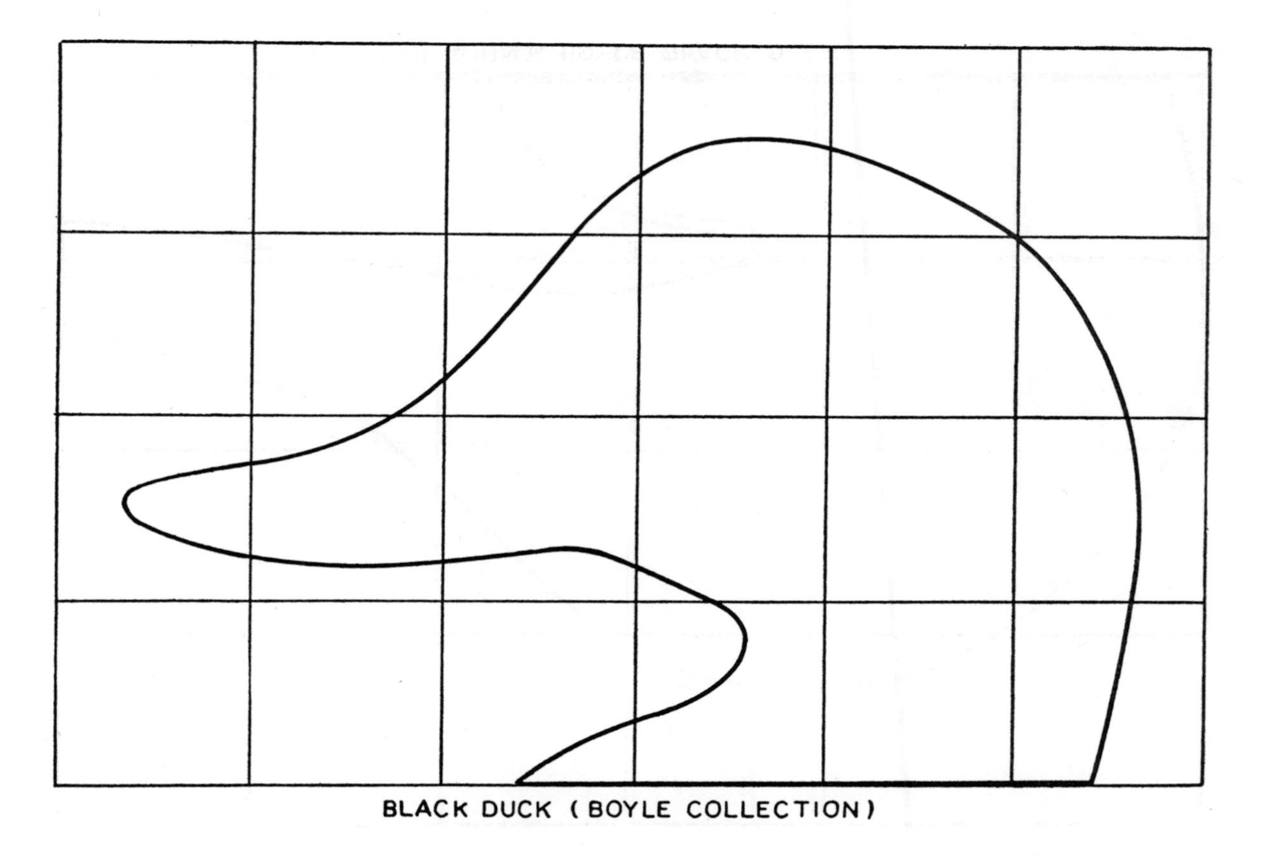

BLACK DUCK (BOYLE COLLECTION)

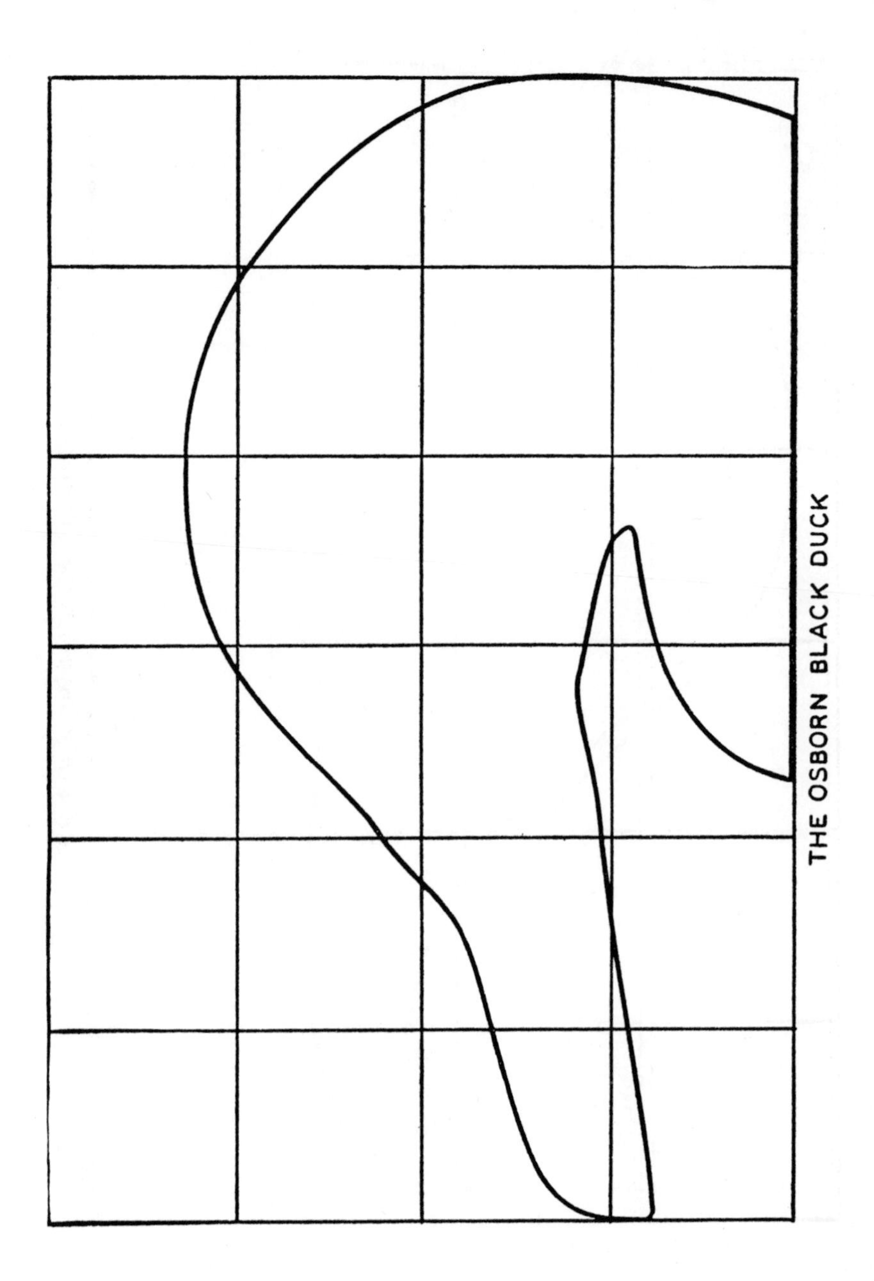
THE OSBORN BLACK DUCK

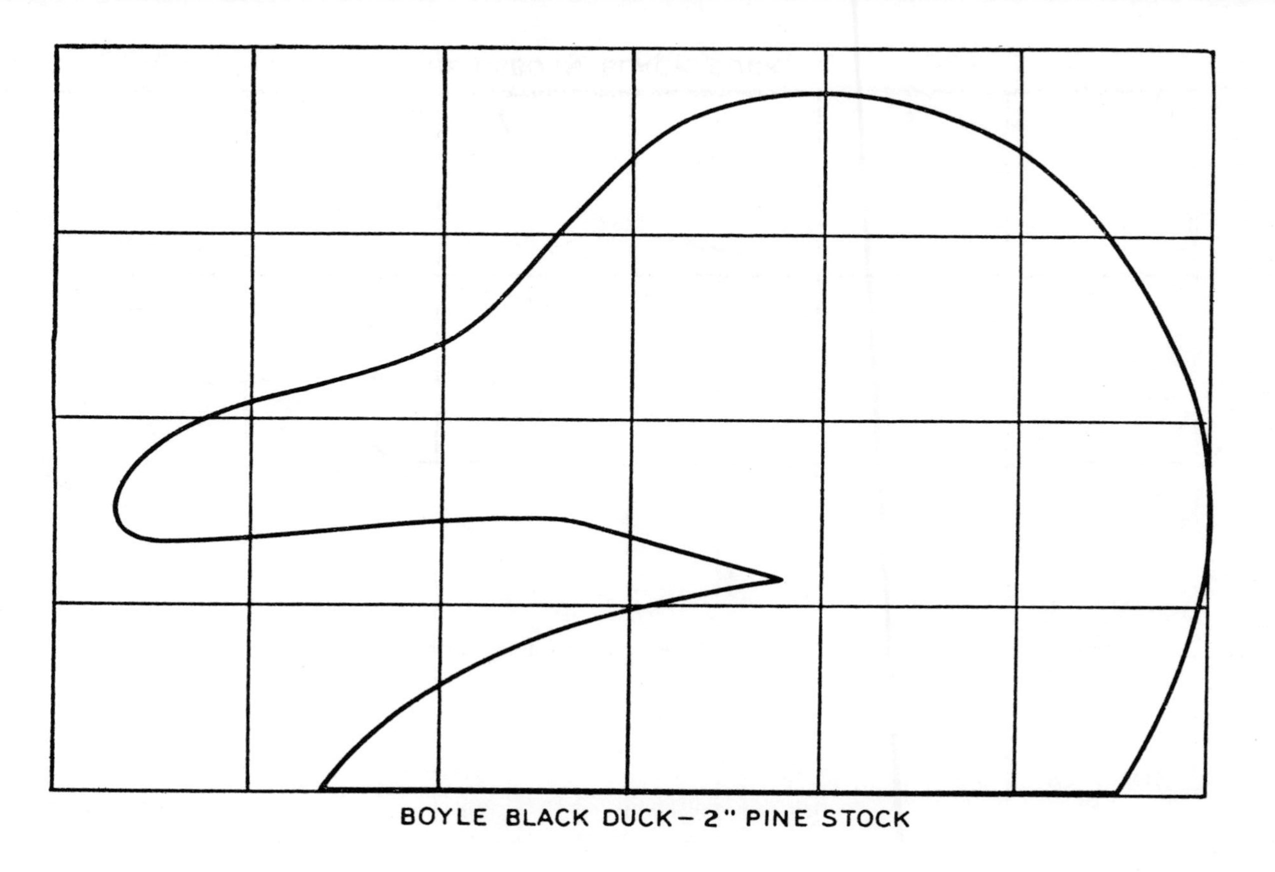
BOYLE BLACK DUCK – 2" PINE STOCK

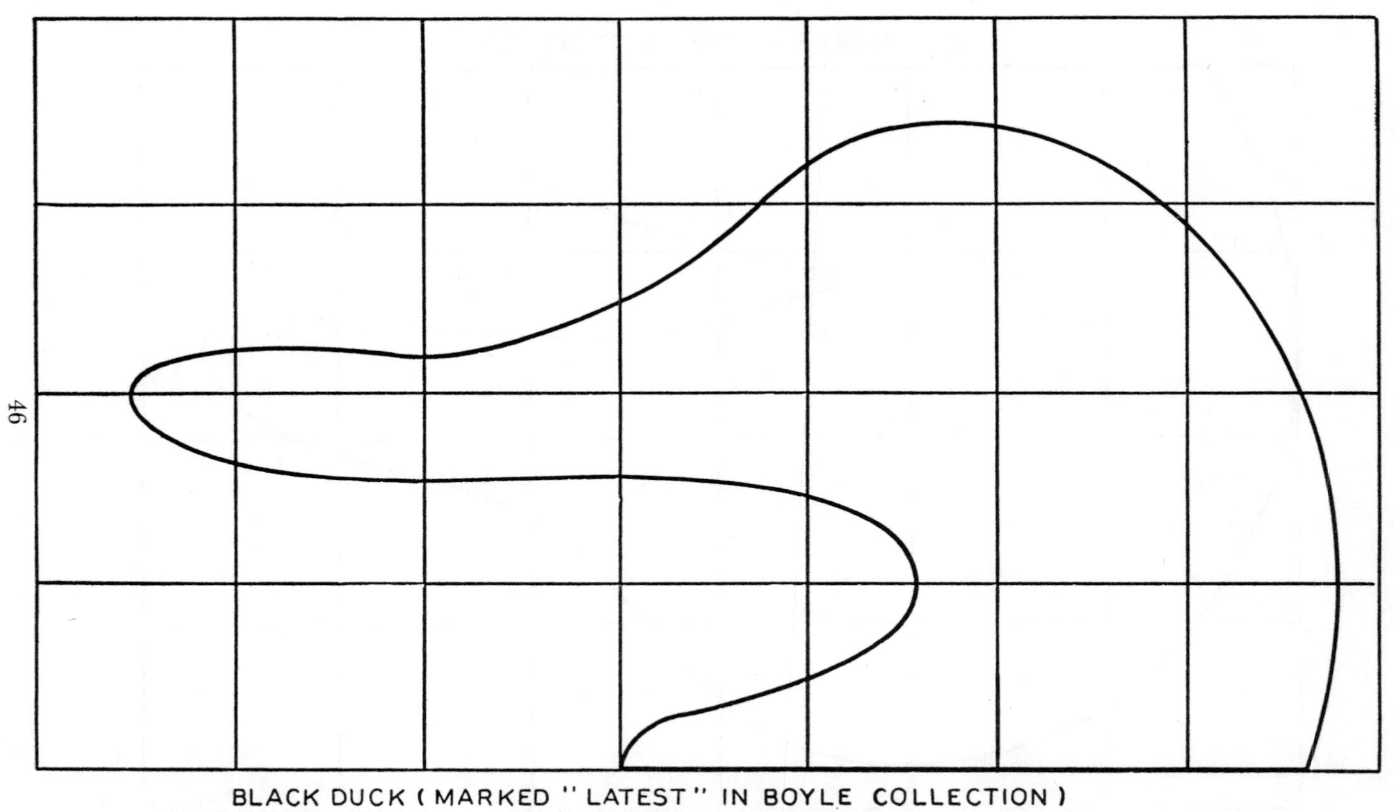

BLACK DUCK (MARKED " LATEST " IN BOYLE COLLECTION)

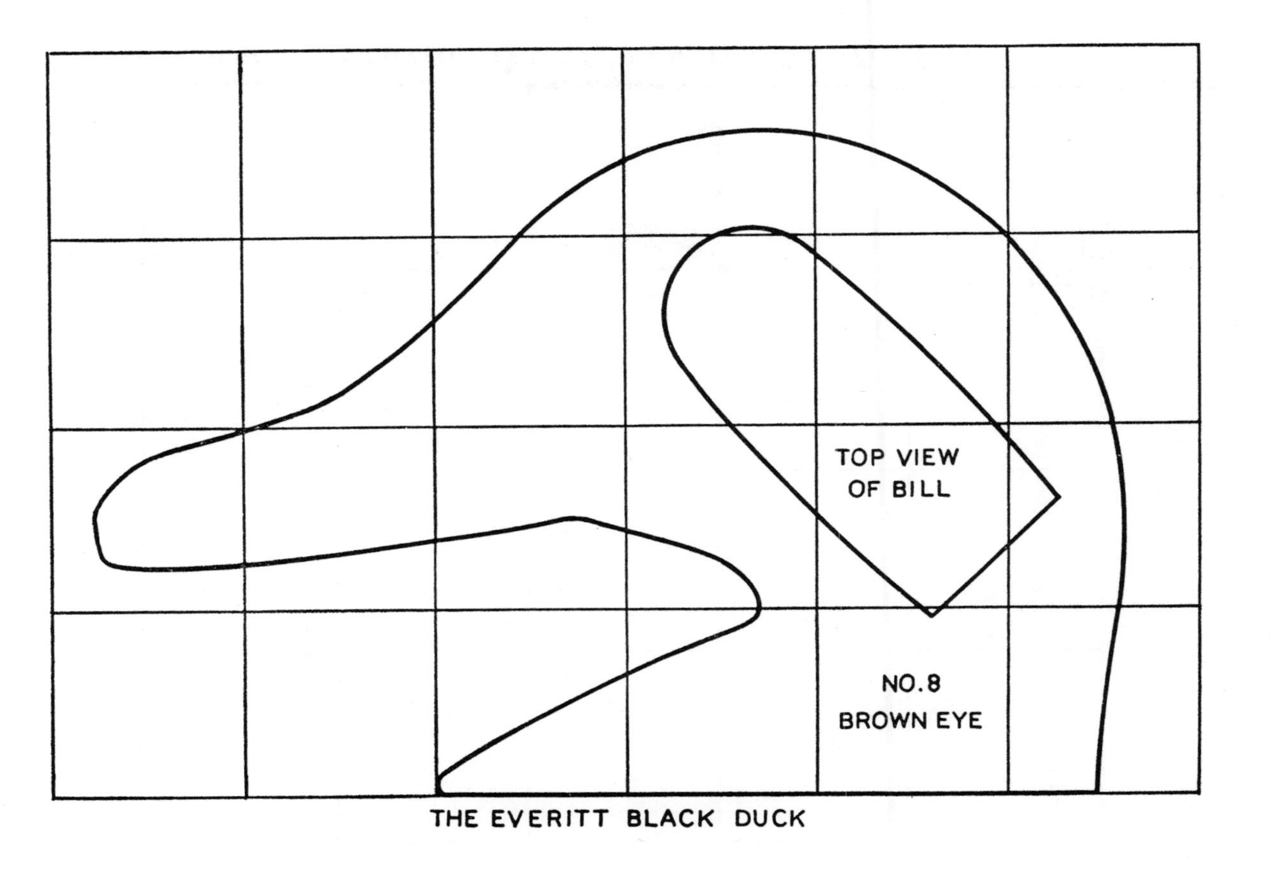

THE EVERITT BLACK DUCK

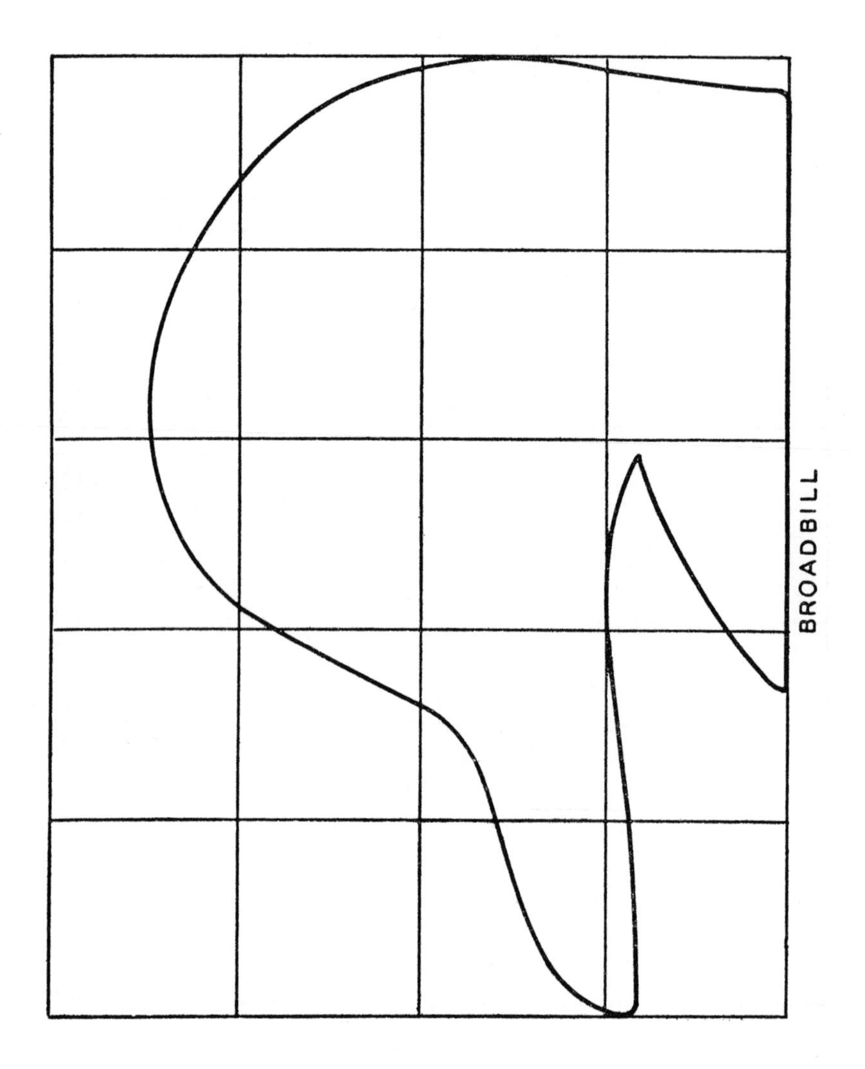
BROADBILL

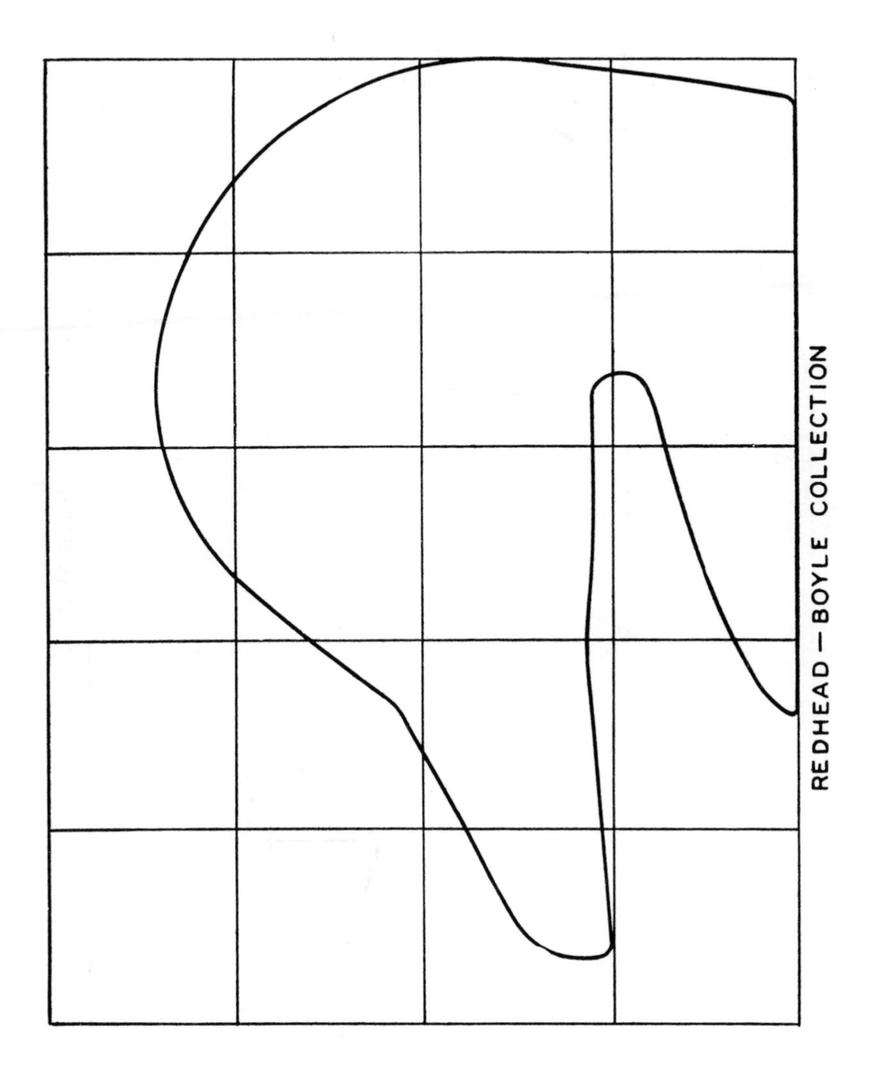
REDHEAD — BOYLE COLLECTION

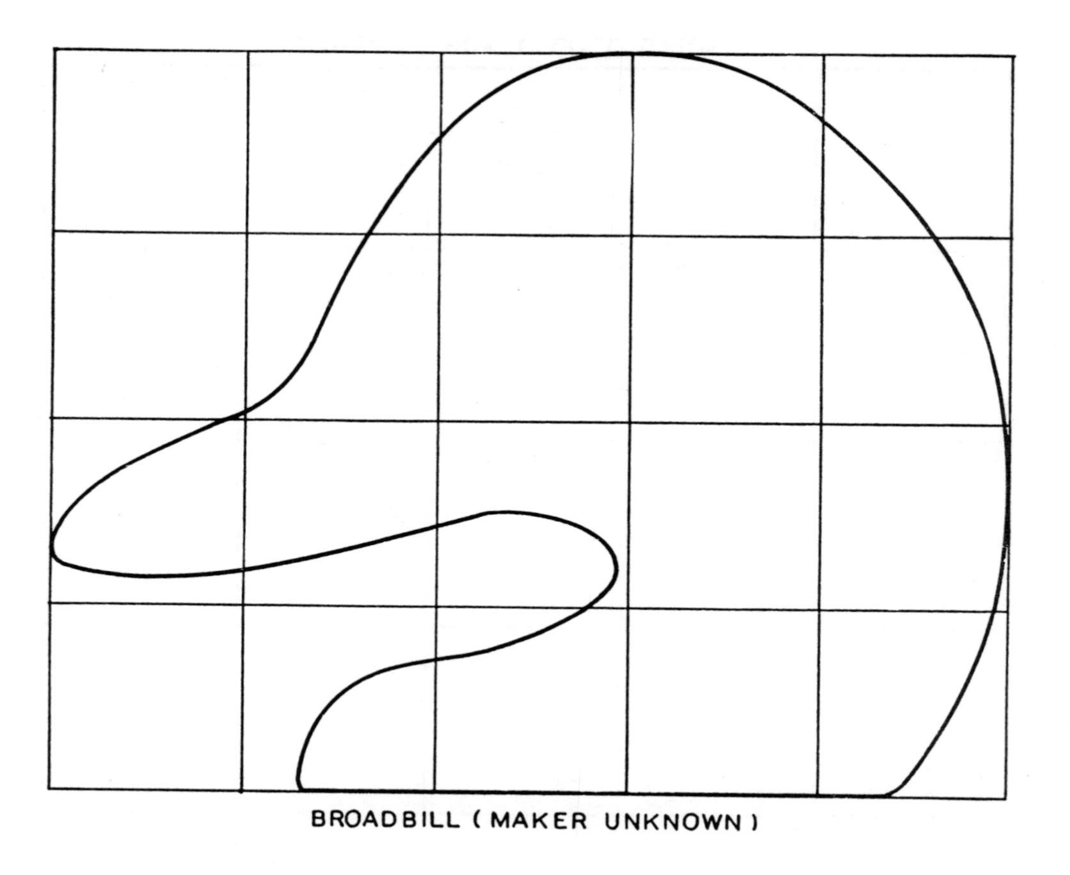

BROADBILL (MAKER UNKNOWN)

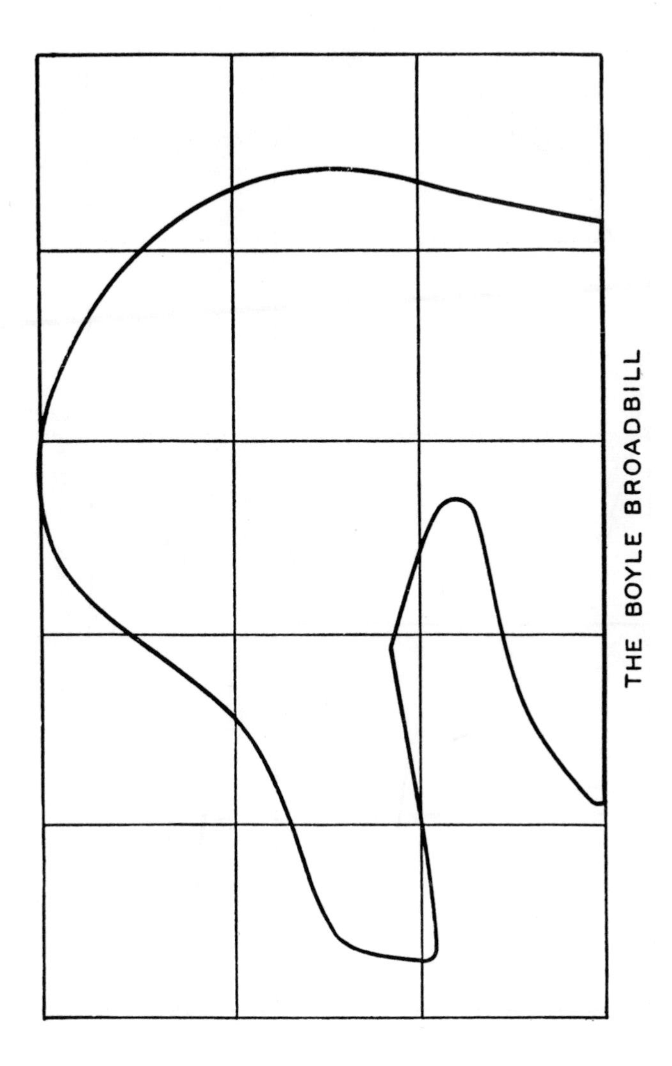

THE BOYLE BROADBILL

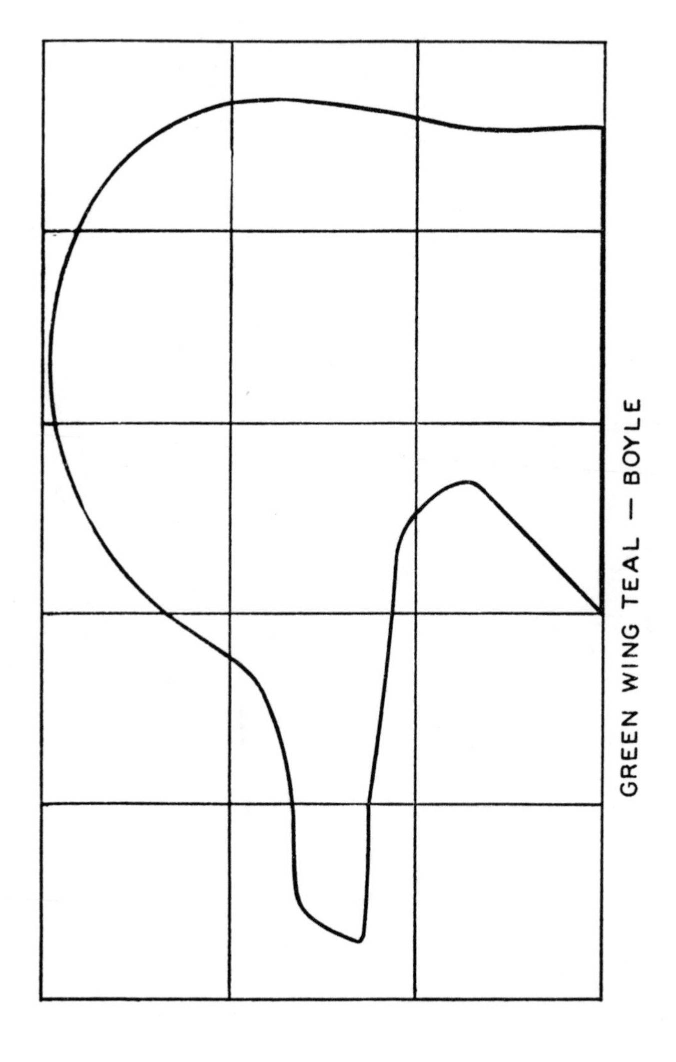

GREEN WING TEAL — BOYLE

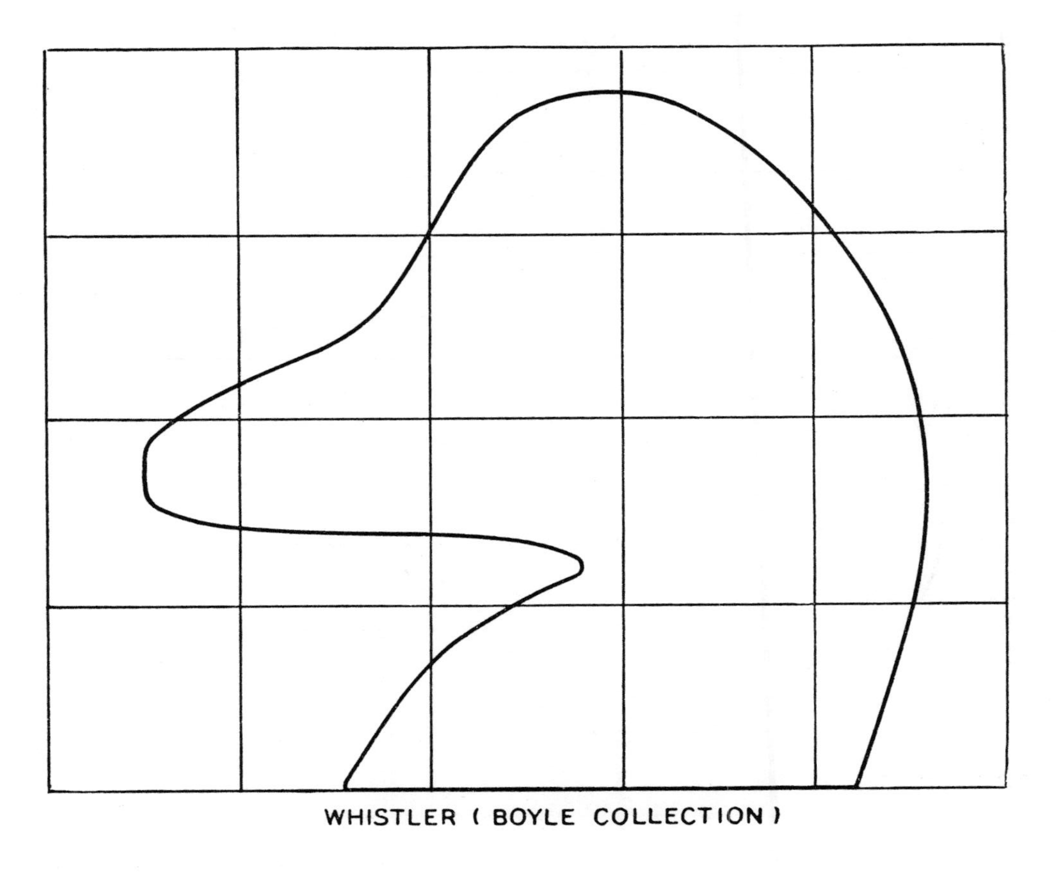

WHISTLER (BOYLE COLLECTION)

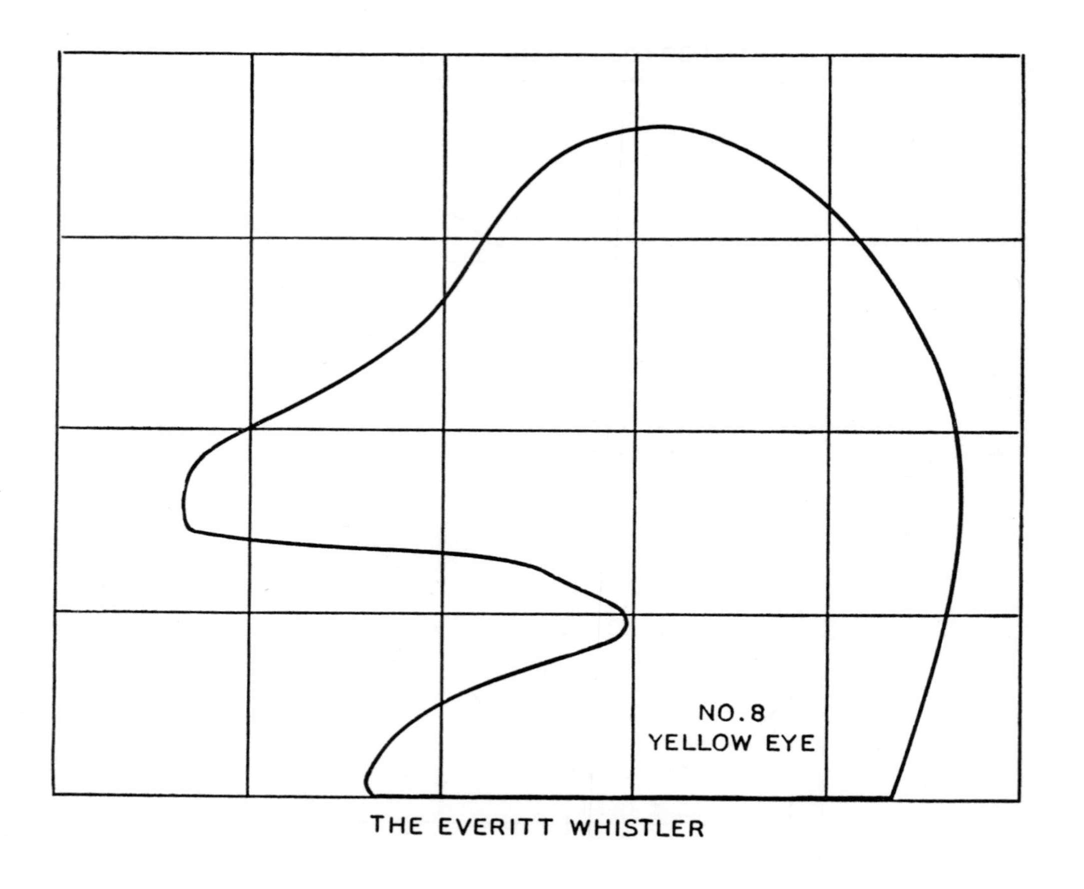

THE EVERITT WHISTLER

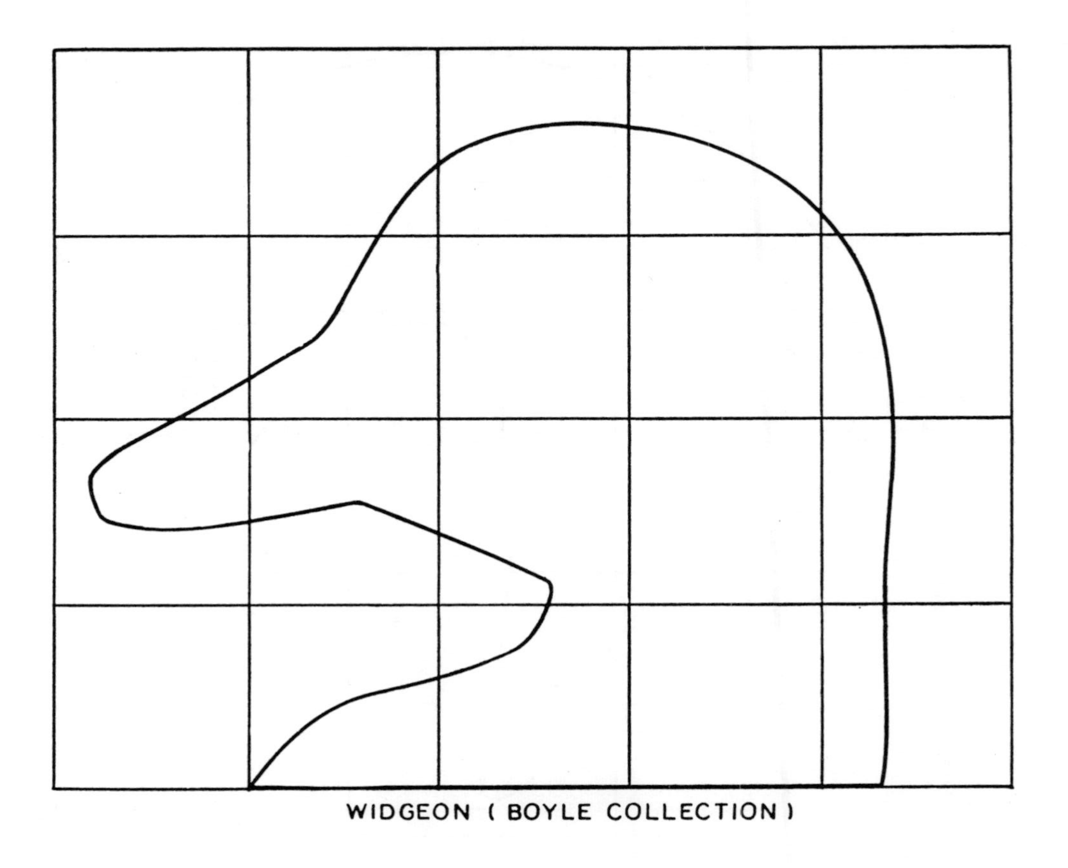

WIDGEON (BOYLE COLLECTION)

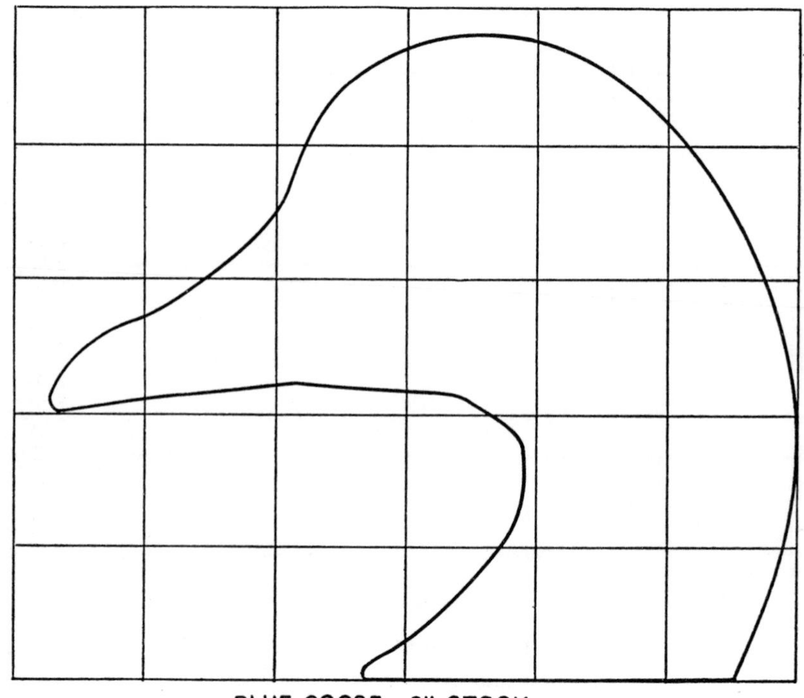

BLUE GOOSE—3" STOCK

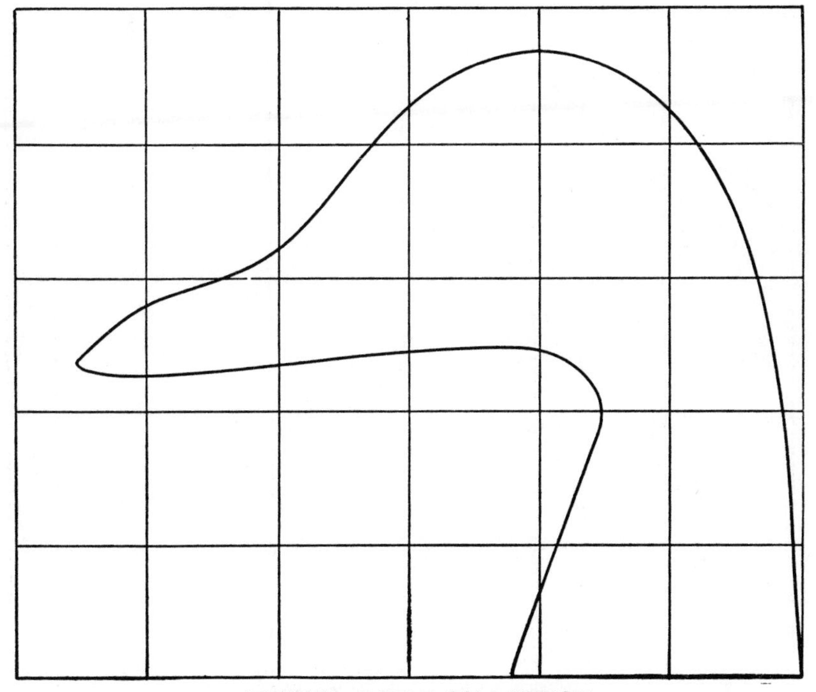

PINTAIL-BOYLE COLLECTION

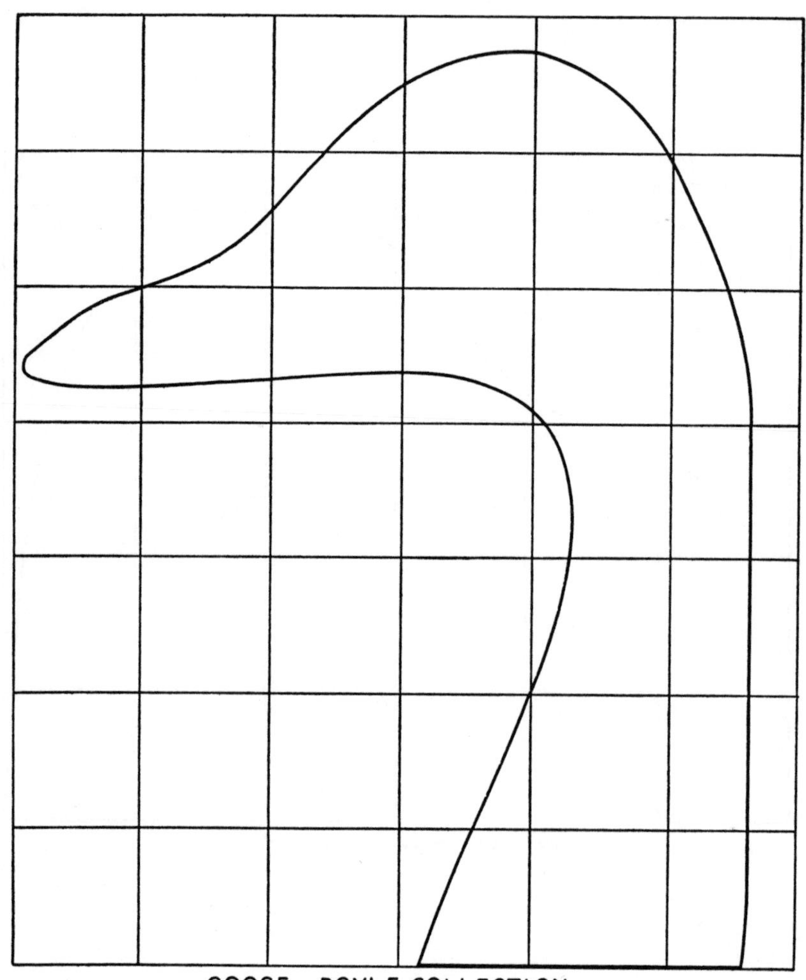

GOOSE – BOYLE COLLECTION

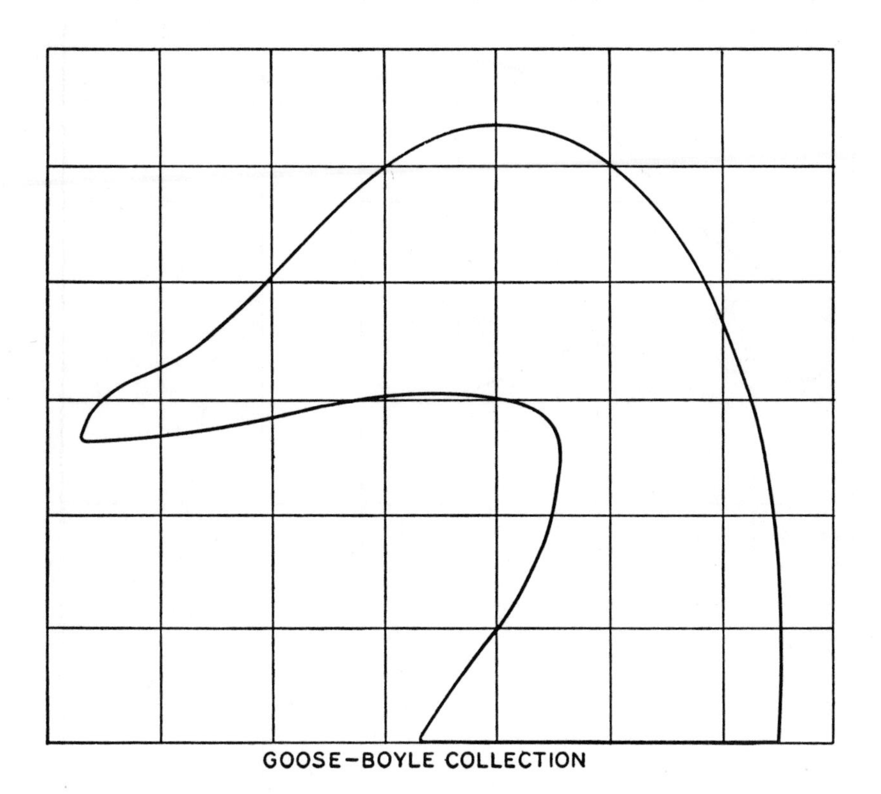

GOOSE—BOYLE COLLECTION

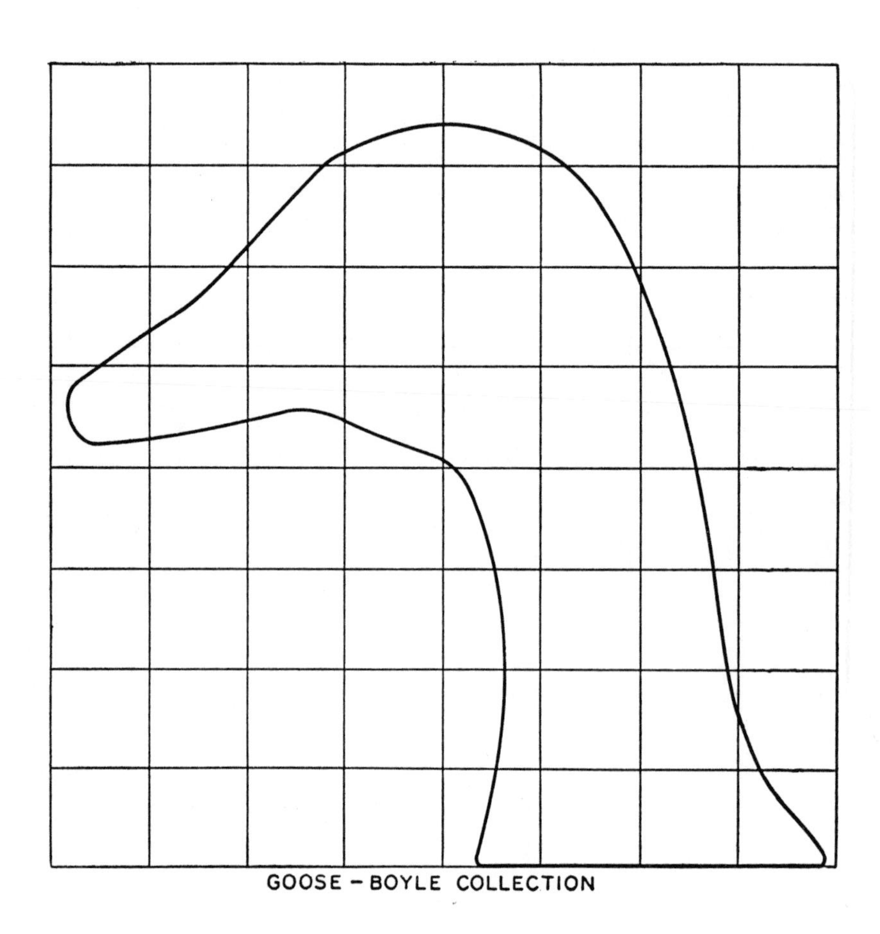

GOOSE – BOYLE COLLECTION

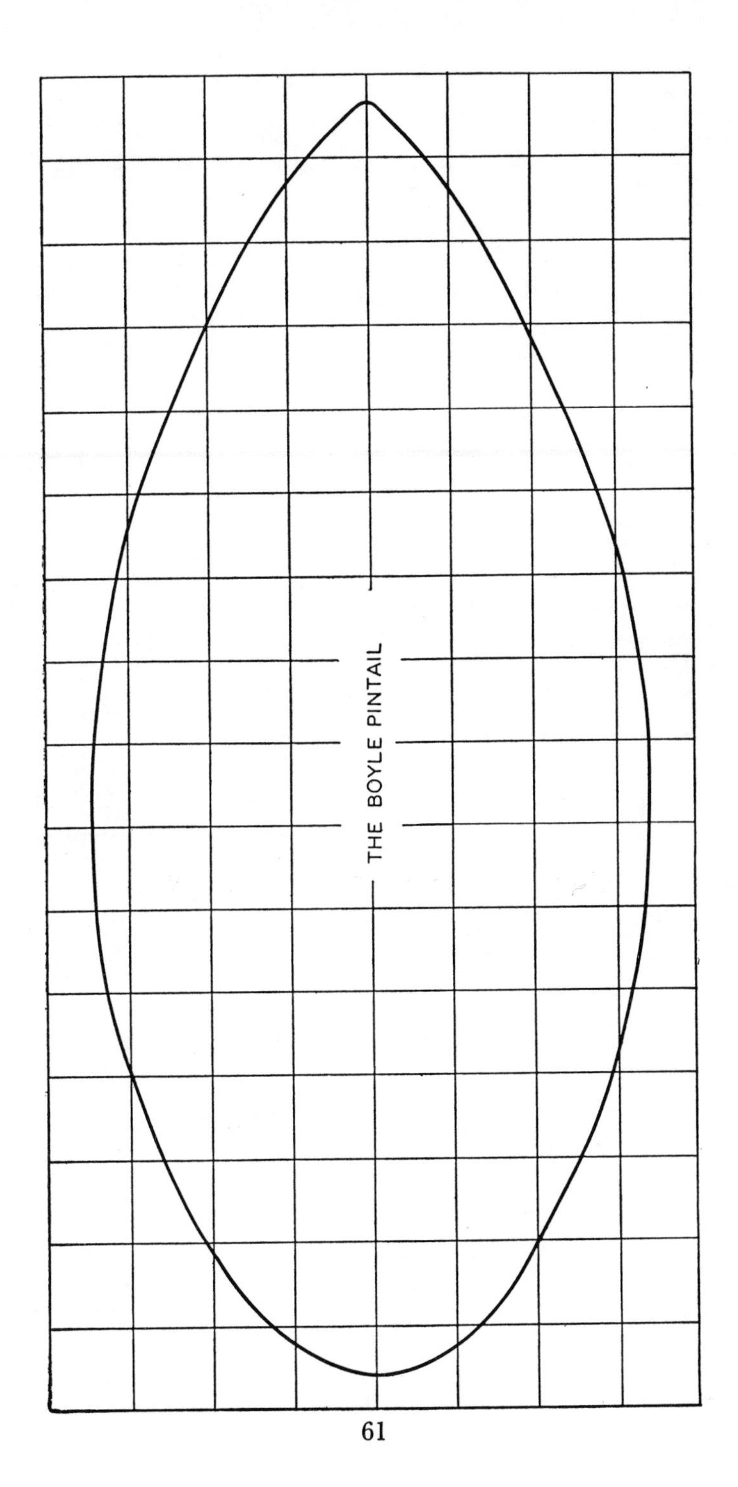
THE BOYLE PINTAIL

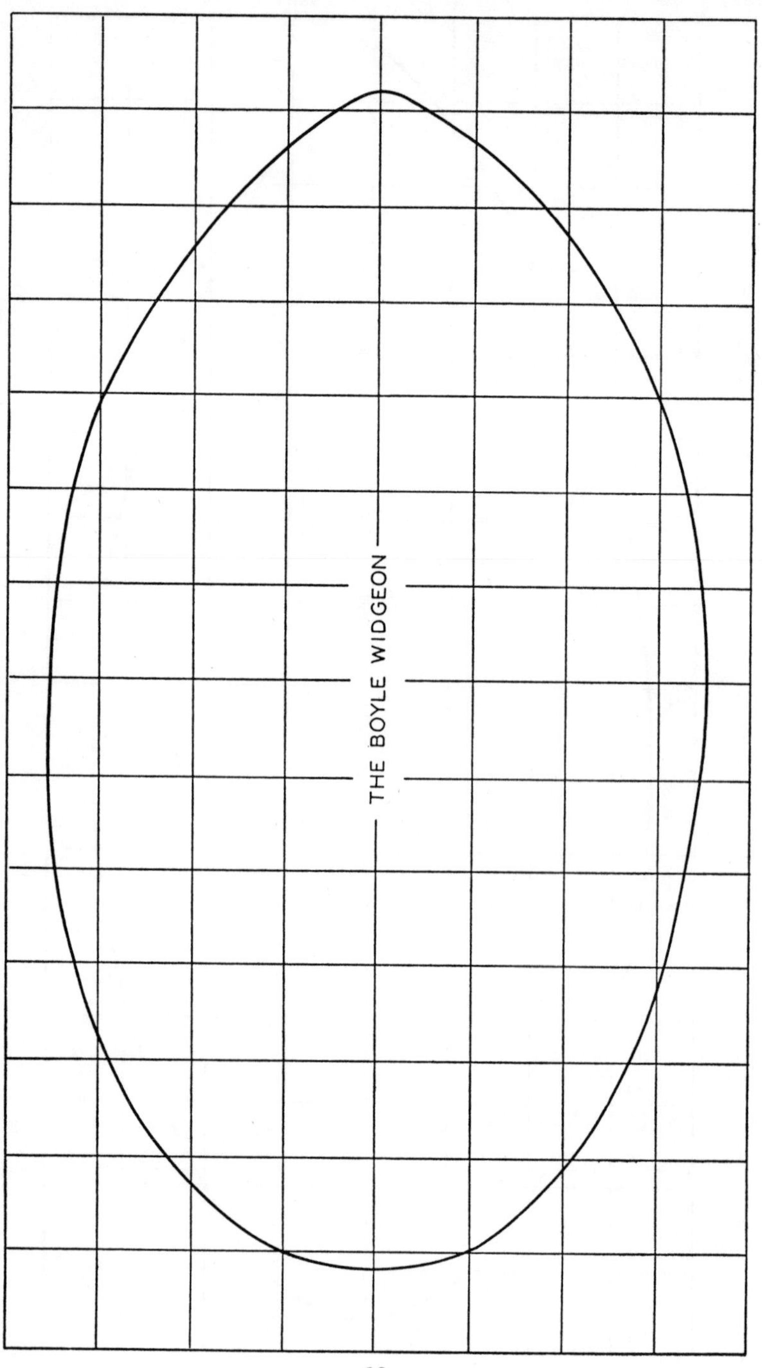
THE BOYLE WIDGEON

Dr. Edgar Burke

COLOR PATTERNS FOR DECOYS

CANADA GOOSE	BRANT
WIDGEON (Male)	WIDGEON (Female)
SURF SCOTER (Male)	SURF SCOTER (Female)
AMERICAN SCOTER (Male)	AMERICAN SCOTER (Female)

Dr. Edgar Burke

COLOR PATTERNS FOR DECOYS

BROADBILL (Male)	BROADBILL (Female)
REDHEAD (Male)	REDHEAD (Female)
CANVASBACK (Male)	CANVASBACK (Female)
GOLDENEYE (Male)	GOLDENEYE (Female)

CHAPTER VII
Body Construction

Solid Wood

This type of body when made of good wood and with sharp tools, need not be difficult. Lay the pattern on the block of wood and draw the outline. If a jig saw of sufficient capacity is available, use it to cut the body to the shape of the pattern. Otherwise use a scroll saw. By carefully laying out the pattern on a piece of wood, it is often possible to get more bodies than would be obtained by merely cutting the wood into lengths as long as the pattern. Tip the pattern this way and that if there is any chance of gaining an extra body, as it is not essential that the grain run fore and aft for a solid wood decoy. Keep your eye open for pieces that will make good heads.

After the plank has been cut to pattern, go to work with a draw knife and begin to shape it. At some point a wood rasp will be more effective. Keep taking off some here and some there, constantly inspecting the body as you go along. In the case of shoal water ducks be very careful not to cut away much depth at the tail end, as you will want this to stick up as high as the wood will allow. Also be chary about reducing the depth of the body about halfway back from the breast. The wings, when folded over the body, make this part of the bird appear high. The forward end of the body, where the head is attached, is quite a bit lower than the middle of the back.

In the case of deep water ducks, the highest point on the

body will be half way back from the breast. From there aft, the body will slant down to within an inch of the waterline. The portion where the head will be attached will not be as low as in the case of the shoal water ducks, but the head will be set on much lower than on the latter. Canvasback can have heads with longer necks than broadbill which should show almost no neck.

When the body has been worked down to shape with a draw knife and rasp, use sandpaper to smooth it off—not too smooth, by the way.

Solid wood decoys can be made of balsa wood if it is possible to obtain the best grade in the required dimensions. The wood is so soft that it must be mounted on a bottom board by gluing and doweling as described under pressed cork decoys. Nails and screws don't hold well in this very soft wood which can be dented with your finger nail. It is almost impossible to get a smooth finish on balsa wood, and this is all to the good as it reduces the shine which a smooth finish decoy tends to have when wet—no matter how flat the paint with which it is covered. Balsa is difficult to work, is very "tender," and better suited to deep water species which lack the raised tails of the shoal water ducks. I have never had occasion to make decoys of balsa wood but I have seen some very nice ones.

Hollow Wood

The tools required consist of a jig saw capable of cutting 1¾" thick wood; a grinder with a cylindrical sandpapering head; a rasp and a medium coarse bastard file. The ancient mainstay of the old time decoy maker, namely a jack knife is not needed when the above tools are available, but a draw knife is useful. A brace with a 1½" extension bit, a chisel, a screw driver, and some sandpaper comprise the chief tools required.

The material used is 2″ white pine, or cedar, dressed down to 1¾″ thick; some ⅜″ hard wood dowels; 2½″ No. 8 and 1″ No. 6 or 8 galvanized or Everdure screws. The bottom of the decoys are made of ½″ wood of the same kind as the body, or of ⅜″ marine plywood. A can of plastic wood is useful in finishing off neck joints.

The first step is to mark out the 1¾″ plank with your pattern in such a way as to obtain as many body sections and heads as possible. In laying out the heads be sure that the grain of the wood runs lengthwise with the bills. The grain will then run across the necks, but as the latter are strengthened with the ⅜″ dowel, this does not matter. Then cut out two sections of the plank as marked out from the pattern.

The two sections for the body are temporarily fastened together with two screws driven in through the bottom section near the center, and clamped in a woodworker's vise. The first rough shaping is done with a draw knife and a rasp, and later smoothed out on the sander sleeve or with the coarse file. Before separating the two pieces "register" marks are made with a pencil at various points around the body so that they may be later fitted together in the exact position in which they were shaped.

If you are making a shoal water duck, the underside of the rear end of the body is cut away to leave a tail extending several inches. Back of where the head will be attached a groove may be sanded or rasped to indicate the division between the folded wings, but this is not essential, although it does add a lifelike touch. The breast will be worked down 1½″ lower than the high point on the back. The plan view of the body will follow the line of the pattern; the elevation will be lower at the breast and place of head attachment; highest half way back; then it drops down a bit, and rises again at the after end of the tail, in the case of shoal water decoys.

Diving ducks will follow the plan of the pattern, and in elevation will be a bit lower at the breast and place of head attachment; then rise at the middle of the back and gradually slope to within an inch of the waterline. On these species the body is left very full amidships. If the decoys are to be used in deep water and will have long anchor lines that must be wound around the body when picking up, make the sides of the body almost parallel through the central half section so that the anchor lines won't have as much tendency to slip off the tail of the body. The decoy thus made will not look quite as natural as a rounded and tapered body, but it will save you untold agony on an icy day when picking up—or setting out—a large rig.

When the two pieces forming the body are fairly well shaped, the lower piece is marked out for hollowing in such a manner that about one inch of side wall is left for holding the long screws which are used for fastening the two pieces together. Leave the walls at the breast and tail thicker than the sides to discourage any tendency to split, and to provide a good solid section for the head. Then bore a hole near the marked out edge of the lower piece of the body and rig the blade of the jig saw through it. The inside of the lower body piece is then cut out.

The underside of the upper half of the body is hollowed out by boring 1½″ holes close together, and then clearing it out with a chisel. Be careful not to bore these holes so deep that the point of the bit goes through the top of the body.

In hollowing out the forward end of the body let me repeat that you must be sure not to go too far toward the front of the breast, as you will need solid wood in that area when it comes time to bore a hole for the dowel which holds the head in place.

Another way to make a hollow body is to hollow out both the top and the bottom sections with a gouge, or the brace

The jig saw and grinding head with sanding sleeve are driven by the same motor, which is mounted on a sliding base.

Upper left is middle body section; upper right is top section. The head rests on bottom board.

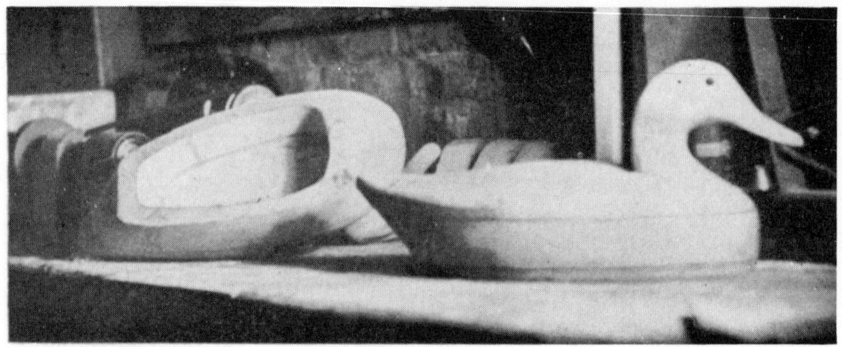

Left-hand decoy is ready for bottom board. Right-hand one has been glued and screwed together.

On left is sawed out head. Center, is head roughed out on sander. Right, the finished head with eyes.

Joint of head and body has been finished with plastic wood on left-hand decoy. Decoy on right has been joined but not yet finished.

and bit and chisel. In this case no bottom piece will have to be added to close the bottom of the body. This makes a slightly less buoyant decoy and one which doesn't have quite as thick a body from top to bottom.

The next step is to coat the edges of both pieces of the body with seam cement or marine glue, carefully fit them together as indicated by the register marks you made earlier, when shaping the body, and clamp them together tightly in a woodworker's vise. Leave the body in the vise for at least 24 hours, to give the glue plenty of time to set up hard. When setting in the vise be sure to protect the relatively soft wood from the jaws of the vise so as not to leave unsightly indentations in the wood.

When the two sections of a glued body have been set up tight, bore holes and countersink them to take the long screws that will hold the body together permanently. These screws should be spaced about 2½″ apart all around the body. If seam cement instead of waterproof glue has been used, bore the screw holes and set up the screws as tightly as possible when the two sections have been secured in the vise. Some of the cement will squeeze out of the joint but this can be scraped off and then sandpapered when dry. If the joint is not perfectly tight and there are any small cavities in the edges of the joint, fill them with plastic wood; allow this to thoroughly harden and file off smooth, fairing up with sandpaper to get a nice, even finish.

Before the bottom piece can be glued and screwed in place, the head must be put on. The making and finishing of heads will be discussed later. Place the head on the body and decide whether it will look best turned to one side or the other—or even turned back in a sleeping position. At least half of the rig should have heads turned one way or the other, and the other half with heads straight ahead. Sleepers' heads can be made from my flat-necked pattern; but if you use only one pattern, the neck on a regular head may be shortened and the head turned backwards and a little to one side.

When you have chosen the position for the head, draw a line around the base of the neck on the top of the body. Then cut out a depression about 1/4″ deep with a small sharp chisel, so that the bottom of the neck will fit neatly into it. This serves two purposes; it makes a stronger joint and prevents the head from twisting out of position. In finishing the shape of the neck and breast make an even profile so that when painted the joint between head and body will not show. Plastic wood can be helpful at this point.

Now for the only difficult part of making a hollow wood decoy: clamp the head in position with a C clamp, the top end of which is fairly well forward on the top of the head, and the lower end of the clamp against the bottom of the breast. Protect the top of the head with a piece of cloth. Then place the whole thing in a vise in such a position that you can bore a 3/8″ hole up through the body and into the head. Watch the depth of the boring so that the point of the bit does not come up through the top of the head. Draw lines on the neck as a guide so that when you have bored through the neck the hole will be as near the center of it as possible. Take your time, keep calm and cuss as much as necessary, if it relieves your feelings. There may be a better way to get this important hole bored correctly through the body and head, but I don't happen to know about it. I have bored the head hole first and then tried to bore the body hole to suit it, but I never had much luck that way. Do the job any way you want, but be sure that the hole goes up through the center of the neck, and that when you put the dowel through body and neck the two come together properly and in the position planned.

At this point I should mention that the most popular way of handling the head dowel is to clamp the blocked-out head, before any shaping has been done, in a vise. This provides two flat sides on the head for secure holding in the vice. Then the dowel hole can be readily bored into the head at the desired angle. But the catch here is that the desired angle is not known at such an early stage in making a really fine decoy. If all heads are to be stuck on bodies at the same angle and in the same position, this easy method of boring is fine; but when each head is to be fitted on at a different angle and in a different position, I feel that the dowel hole should be bored at the time this position is determined—after the body and the head have been almost finished.

When the hole is bored, coat a hard wood dowel with casein glue, and pour some more down through the hole in the head. Then insert the dowel and work it up until it reaches to the top of the hole in the head. Cut off the dowel even with the bottom of the body. Leave the whole thing in the C clamp until the glue has set up hard. When the glue has set up fill in around the bottom of the neck with plastic wood if necessary to give a nice smooth finish to the joint between the head and body. When hard, smooth it with a file and some sandpaper. Take some pains to get a natural looking joint here—many decoys look as though the head and body were two separate pieces just stuck together. Make yours look all in one piece, like a live duck.

The next step is to place the body on a piece of ½″ pine or ⅜″ marine plywood, and draw the outline of the body on the bottom piece. Cut this out on the jig saw. Before attaching this piece, paint the inside of the body with lead and oil paint—any old color. Then bore holes and countersink them for the 1″ screws that will hold the bottom board in place, first having coated the joint with seam cement. If glue is to be used, give it plenty of time to set up before boring the holes. It is wise to note the positions of the long screws already set in the upper part of the body, marking them with a pencil so that you won't be tempted to try to bore your new holes into those screws. Paint the inside side of the bottom board before screwing and gluing in place.

You can now put the finishing touches on your decoy, viewing it from all angles, and smoothing it out here and there, fairing up the lines. A keel may be attached by screwing it in place with screws that won't go through the thin bottom board, but this should be left to do until after the bottom has one, or preferably two coats of paint. Longer screws can be used in the breast and tail sections which have not been hollowed out. Be sure that the keel is firmly attached, because the anchor line will be fastened to it through a hole near the forward end, and there can be a heavy strain on it in rough weather.

Natural Cork

The traditional and correct way to build up a natural cork body is to fasten the pieces together with dowels, inserted at opposing angles to prevent the pieces from pulling apart. Although glue was not used, and is not necessary, it is good practice to coat the dowels and the pieces of cork where they join with a waterproof marine glue.

Cork decoys are made without bottom boards, the keel being the chief strengthening agent. Therefore, we outline the pattern on the bottom piece of cork and on a band saw, if one is available, cut the piece out roughly. A hand saw may be used in place of a band saw. Make the bottom section of the body from a single piece of cork; the top section may be constructed of several pieces cut to shape.

It is very important to get a smooth and accurate fit where the cork slabs are joined. You will discover that one side of the cork slab is much smoother than the other. Use the *smooth sides together,* after leveling them off as accurately as possible.

Place the two pieces in a carpenter's vise and tighten up

until the cork is compressed to some degree. From a cedar shingle fashion a number of dowels, with sharp and long tapered points. The top of the dowel should be made square in section, so that it won't twist when set in the cork. If the diameter of the dowel is 1/4", bore 1/8" holes through the two sections of cork, and drive home the dowels—not straight up and down, but with each pair at an opposing angle, so that they will not pull out. Sink the dowels well into the cork so that further sanding and rasping can be done without cutting them. With rasp and sandpaper shape the body to its rough, general contours.

Now the keel and head must be attached to the body. Two *locust* dowels are used for this purpose—one near the stern end of the body and the other at the forward end to secure the head to the body.

Unless you have a woodworking lathe, you will probably have to make your own locust dowels by hand, as the old Great South Bay decoy makers did—and still do. First work the locust down to the rough shape and size of the dowel. Then drive this through a clean-cut hole which has been bored through a piece of hardened steel. The hole should be of the diameter required for the dowel, about 3/8". This will produce a nice round, even dowel from your roughly shaped wood.

The keel, which should be 1 1/2" deep by 1" thick, of clear white pine, should be carefully shaped to a nice fit against the bottom of the body. You then bore holes through the keel near the forward and rear ends to take the locust dowels. The position of the head dowel near the forward end of the keel, must be such that the head will be in a proper position. The hole for the rear dowel should be drilled so that it will be several inches from the tail end of the body. Both of these holes must be exactly centered through the keel from side to side—this is important!

The rear dowel is the first to be put in place. When this

dowel has been driven home through this hole and a smaller hole through the cork body, see that the top of the dowel is sunk far enough into the cork to permit final shaping and sanding of the top of the body. Cut the lower end off even with the bottom of the keel. Then drill a hole through the keel and the lower end of the dowel to take a copper or galvanized nail. The locust is so tough that you won't be able to drive this nail without first drilling for it.

Next the head dowel is prepared by sawing a small slit in its top end, which will receive a thin pine wedge, the latter being driven home when the head is finally set on the dowel. In making this type of decoy, the hole for the head dowel is bored right through the head from top to bottom, instead of being bored from the bottom up and not all the way through the top of the head. The hole through the keel, and a smaller one through the cork body, will take the head dowel snugly, and the lower end is then secured with a copper or galvanized nail through the keel. Be sure that the top of this dowel is level with the top of the head. I suggest that the head and dowel be made secure with casein glue, rather than the insertion of a pine wedge.

Before finally doweling the head in place, rasp down to shape the top of the forward end of the body so that the head will fit on it smoothly in the desired position. When the head is on and in place, drive two toe nails through the forward base of the neck into the cork body to prevent the head from twisting out of position. It is wise to drill holes for these nails to avoid any possibility of splitting the neck. If you will glance at the black duck head patterns from the Great South Bay, shown elsewhere in this book, you will notice that the forward end of the necks are carried further forward than in the average head; this was to provide for secure toe nailing on cork bodies, among other things.

When the decoy has been completely assembled, give the

body its final shape with a coarse rasp and sandpaper. The best rasp is what is known as a "horse rasp" which has coarser teeth than the usual wood rasp.

Properly constructed cork decoys, made as I have outlined above, will last for many, many years—even if no glue has been used in putting them together, and are, in my opinion, the very best you can have. They are light, buoyant and tough, and if used for black ducks can be burned to an unequaled finish. They can also be readily painted for other species.

Pressed Cork

We start with a bottom board cut out the shape of the desired pattern for the decoy we wish to make, making necessary allowance for an undercut tail. If pressed cork of sufficient thickness can be obtained, it will not be necessary to glue two slabs together. However, if two inch slabs are the best you can get, first cut out several bottom boards and place these on a slab of cork in such a way as to get as many body sections as possible from the slab. Then coat the bottom board liberally with casein glue, letting the glue stand for about an hour before applying it. Be sure to follow instructions on the can in detail, as these glues depend upon a chemical reaction for their efficiency. When the bottom boards have been laid in place, either clamp in a large vice, or put heavy weights on them and let them stand over night or even longer. A board can be laid over the bottom boards and then some heavy stones or any other weights placed on it so that a considerable pressure will be exerted evenly on all the surfaces of the bottom boards.

When the glue has set up hard, you can then cut out each body with an ordinary saw and shape it up roughly with a rasp. If it is necessary to add another thickness of cork lay your pattern over another slab and saw a section out roughly. Then glue this on top of the first section, using plenty of glue and letting it set up under pressure. You could glue two slabs of cork together before cutting out to shape, but I think you would not get as good a bond between the two whole slabs as you will with smaller areas to join.

When the keel has been added drill two holes to take dowels through it, and drive these—covered with glue—up into the body to give additional security to the body.

If you are making shoal water ducks, and therefore want a raised tail, you can give this extended tail added and *most*

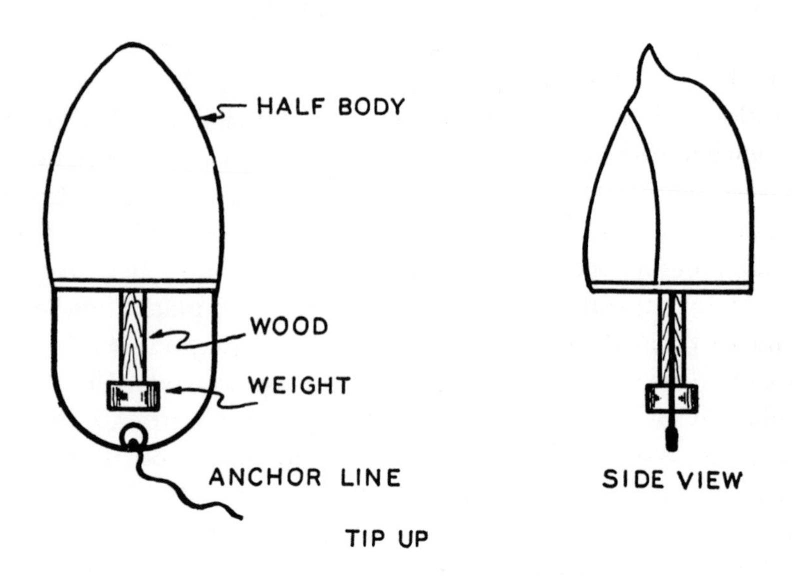

TIP UP

necessary strength by driving a sharpened ⅜″ dowel into the end of the tail and down through the body at an angle until the dowel touches the bottom board. As soon as you feel the dowel touch the bottom board, stop driving it, as you will only pry the board away from the cork if you aren't careful.

The suggestions for shaping the body are the same as those given for making hollow wooden decoys. The heads are put on by boring a hole through the bottom board, driving the dowel up through the cork and into the head, which has been bored to receive it. Use plenty of glue on the dowel and pour some into the hole in the head. Cut the dowel off level with the bottom of the bottom board. In smoothing up the body use rough sandpaper. As many as three or four coats of fairly thick paint can be used for priming the body and filling the small holes in the cork. This, as has been pointed out, will serve as a great protection for the pressed cork body material, and will prevent it from "scuffing off" under rough treatment. Add the keel by screwing or toe nailing to the bottom board.

Tip ups, to imitate feeding ducks, are made as follows: make a half body, the rear half—out of solid cork or wood. It should really be a bit more than a half portion, as it will sink somewhat due to the ballast. Instead of having the bottom of the body flat, as in a regular floating decoy, make it rounded like a live duck. The lower end of the body is cut off square, and a piece of round wood, about 3/4″ in diameter and 5″ long, is inserted into the center of the squared off end. This can be doweled in or securely glued in place. Probably both will be safest. At the lower end of the stick attach a lead ballast of sufficient weight to hold the tail of the tip up in the air when floating. In the case of a solid cork decoy the next step will be made much easier if a "bottom board" has been glued to the squared off end of the body, further secured by several slanted in dowels. This is not necessary if a wooden body is used.

Then take a piece of heavy copper or galvanized wire, long enough so that when it is bent from one side of the body around under the stick with the weight attached and up to the other side of the body, it will clear the weight comfortably. Before securing this wire to the body with staples, slip a tie ring over it, to which the anchor cord will be tied, and fashion a loop in the wire at the lowest point to prevent the ring from sliding.

The tip up is excellent for a rig of black duck. In the case of a flock of mallards, it is probably better to make a mallard decoy body, with the breast slanted down to the surface, as though the duck's head were reaching down to the bottom. This can be painted as a mallard drake, and will show up nicely as a feeding bird. This feeding mallard should not be

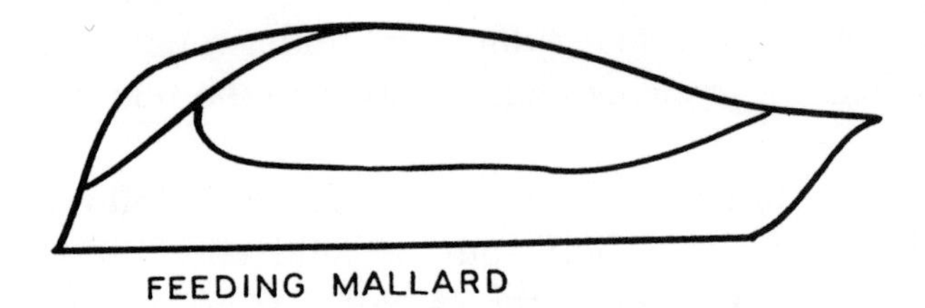

FEEDING MALLARD

used in deep water, because ducks can see the bottom of the water and will readily judge its depth. Mallard tip ups could more easily be made to represent hen birds, which will simplify the painting problem, and work just as well on the live birds.

When setting out tip ups be sure that they lie with their backs to the wind; they will look more natural this way.

CHAPTER VIII

Making Decoy Heads

Many is the head that I have whittled out of a piece of white pine with my jack knife, the traditional way in which those artists of the tidewater marshes slowly but cleverly created a form of sculpture that has now been recognized as valuable early American art. But today you can buy a grinder head for a few dollars, with a sanding sleeve attachment, and with one-half the effort turn out a duck decoy head that is fully the equal of the work done by those old baymen whom men of my generation knew and revered.

In the days of large bag limits, when hundreds of decoys were used with battery rigs, and professional guides needed several hundred shoal water duck decoys for the establishments that flourished along the coast, many woodworking mills would cut out decoy heads for five cents apiece; then it was up to you to whittle them down to the finished article. Today you can buy a power jig saw for less than the price of a dozen first class commercial decoys, and cut the heads out yourself—and even better than the mills did when I was a lot younger.

So I suggest that you invest in a third horse power electric motor, a jig saw and a grinder head with a sanding sleeve attachment. These will make light work out of what once was a slow, tedious and difficult job. And I am so bold as to predict that you will be able to turn out decoy heads of superlative quality, once you get the hang of the thing.

Good patterns for decoy heads are essential, whether you

have a mill cut out the heads or do it yourself. Lay the pattern on a piece of two inch pine when making mallard, black duck or canvasback heads, and draw the outline on the wood. You can use 1½″ wood for the smaller species. Then run this through the jig saw and you have a rough piece with good profile but square edges and no modeling. It is a good plan to cut out a dozen such heads at a time; sooner or later you will find use for them. If you are commercially minded you can always sell the blocked-out heads for a lot more than five cents, and can rest assured that what the other fellow finally makes out of them will be quite different from what you achieve. Each decoy maker has a very distinctive style in finishing out a head, and very few heads lack the individual touch of the maker.

The next step is to round off the corners of the blocked-out head on the sanding sleeve. Problem number one is to make your first model, in the event that you haven't been lucky enough to get a good model from some other source. Work the wood down, making a generous groove on the upper half of each side of the head. Below this will be the bulging cheek, and below that sand out again to the size of the neck. Round off the back of the head and neck, and the front of the neck under the bill. Treat the bill with great care; one false move here and you will never get a good looking head. It is very easy to take too much off the bill. Keep examining the head from all angles as you slowly but surely sand off more and more as you approach the final shape. A medium half round bastard file is useful in the last stages. It is just impossible to tell you in so many words exactly what shape the finished head should have. You will have to look at mounted birds, study the pictures in this book, or follow a first class sample head. The latter can be bought from a commercial decoy maker as a rule. Wildfowler Decoys, Inc., Old Saybrook, Connecticut, usually have heads for sale. If you are inexperienced and have

E. V. Connett

Feeding mallard.

W. H. Voght

Feeding black duck.

Dr. Edgar Burke

Pintail (Male)
Widgeon (Male)

Pintail (Female)
Widgeon (Female)

no model, try to get one from them. It will be a good one. Later on you can develop your own fine points in sculpturing your heads.

You will need your knife (sharp!) when modeling the line where the bill meets the head. This is a very important feature and must be done skillfully. See top and views of decoys in Dr. Burke's black and white plates.

When you have finally sanded down the head by hand and are satisfied with it, you are ready to put in the eyes. First mark the spot where each eye goes, being sure that these are opposite each other. The commonest mistake is placing the eyes too high in the head. Just above the bulge of the cheek is right.

Each glass eye comes on a wire several inches long. Clip this wire off to about 5/8″ and with small round nosed pliers make an open loop of this—like a fish hook. Now bore a hole that will take the eye snugly and deep enough so that when your loop of wire is seated in the hole the glass eye will protrude about 1/32 at the top. *See that the eye is straight up and down and not slanted in at the top.* Now put some plastic wood in the hole, enough to fill it when the eye is inserted, and push the eye into position. When the plastic wood is hardened the eye will never come out. Immediately clean any plastic wood off the eye before it hardens!

That's all there is to it.

Almost every species of duck has a distinctive head and bill. A widgeon with the bill of a black duck would be an abortion. And vice versa. Years ago I tried to make some decoy heads for an unfamiliar species by studying the pictures in a bird book. It just didn't work. A mounted bird, or a bird you have shot, is the best model. Remember that even the bird artists often miss the distinctive pose and character of many ducks. Really strive to perfect the heads of your decoys. As I have said elsewhere, a fine head on a mediocre body is better than a fine body with a poor head—in my opinion, of course.

The various species of waterfowl not only have differently shaped heads but carry them differently when resting on the water. I have spoken of the fact that nervous ducks raise their heads, while peaceful birds are inclined to carry their heads sunk down to their bodies. But there is still a characteristic head carriage for the different species, even when they are not upset. Resting broadbill show no neck whatever; mallards and black ducks show very little neck; canvasbacks show some neck, and pintails show the most. An experienced gunner could look at an unpainted and well designed decoy and unerringly tell whether it was a shoal water or deep-water bird; whether it was a broadbill or canvasback; whether it was a pintail or a widgeon. And he would arrive at his decisions by the properly delineated shape and carriage of the head, to say nothing of the body.

It is my belief that wildfowl not only distinguish their own species by their distinctive coloration, but also by the conformation of the head and body, and the carriage of the head. I am fully aware of the fact that ducks have come in to lumps of mud and tin cans; but I am equally aware of the fact that under present day conditions—and especially when native birds have been shot at a few times—the lumps of mud and tin cans won't bring any self-respecting black duck, pintail or widgeon within four gunshots. It is difficult enough to toll such birds within gunshot with the very finest decoys.

If we are going to the trouble of making a set of fine decoys, we might just as well get not only the bodies, heads and coloring right, but also the characteristic pose of the unworried bird. The accompanying sketches will be of assistance to you in incorporating this feature into your decoys.

For wooden decoys don't finish the bottom of the neck off

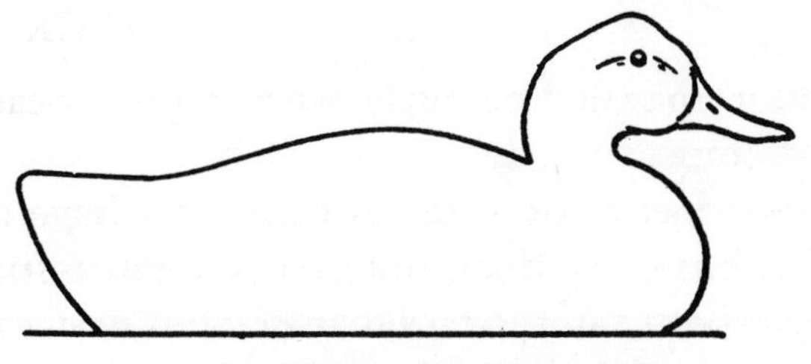

BLACK DUCK OR MALLARD

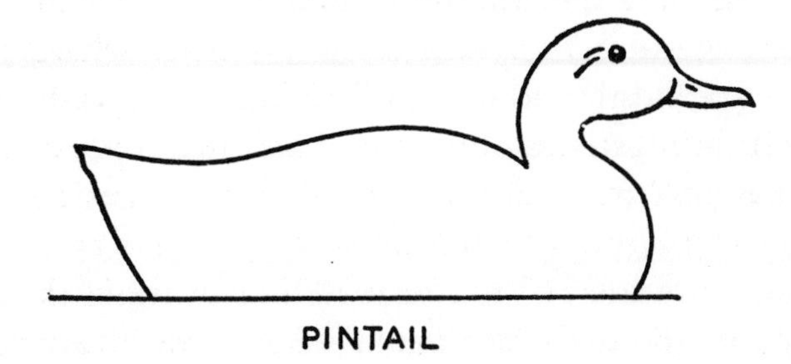

PINTAIL

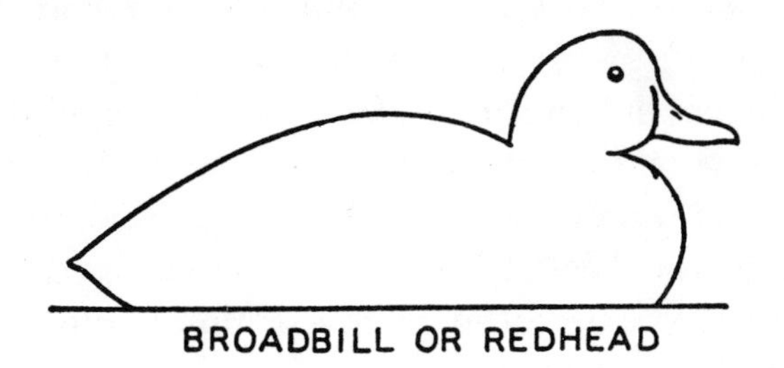

BROADBILL OR REDHEAD

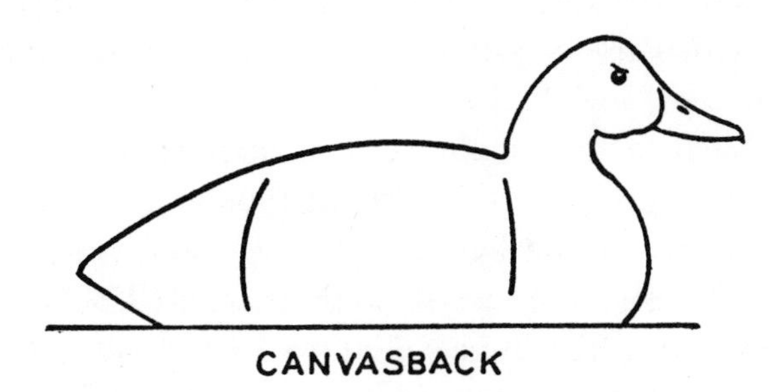

CANVASBACK

in a beautifully rounded curve; leave about an eighth of an inch squared up at the base of the neck. This can be fitted into a corresponding slot cut in the body, in any position that the head is to have. Such a plan will provide a very strong and durable arrangement for attaching the head to the body, and will avoid any tendency for the head to twist around, in case the glue on the dowel lets go. It also avoids the necessity of driving a nail through the neck and into the dowel or the body to hold the head tightly in position. This nailing can split a fine head, and cause other kinds of trouble. Avoid it by carefully mortising the base of the head into the body. I know that this isn't easy, but it is worth doing and doing right. Add casein glue to the mortise and base of the head.

I have already covered that fearful adventure of boring the dowel hole in the body and head. There just must be a way of doing this easily, but in many long years I have never discovered it. An expert with a drill press—which I don't own—might be able to solve this problem for you. By the way, I have bored the hole from the top of the head down through the neck and into the body; that is not so difficult. But sooner or later the dowel may swell or work up above the top of the head unless a wedge is used and the dowel nailed through the keel. Sometimes the dowel will shrink and leave a cavity where the duck's brain should be. And that looks awful. The right way to do the job is from below so that the top of the dowel is inside the top of the head.

One last word on heads: I would rather have them a bit bigger than they should be, rather than smaller. The head and neck of a live duck looks very skinny. If you made your decoy heads this small they would not look right. Lean toward the large side in making heads.

I think it pays to cut the nostrils in a duck's bill, rather than merely paint them on. Don't make them too big. If you wish to indicate the joint between the upper and lower half of the bill, get the right wood carving tool and do so. All these little touches add to the appearance of the decoy —in your hand, if not on the water. It is often a sore temptation to try to carve feathers, etc. on the body of a decoy. An indication of the wings along the side of the tail end of the decoy can be a help in painting, but other carving of that sort really doesn't belong on a decoy that is to get hard usage, and I am sure that wild birds will not appreciate it as much as your admiring friends. Keep your decoys practical and able to take the beating to which they will be exposed.

CHAPTER IX

Painting Decoys

Some men have a knack with brushes and paints, and other men don't. I have friends who can turn out a beautiful decoy up to the point of painting it. Then they just don't seem to be able to carry on. I have other friends who can paint a decoy nicely but simply can't turn out a decent body and head, nor put them together so that they will stay put. Fortunately there are two styles of painting decoys and for many long years the birds have been coming to both of them.

The first style we will call the bayman's painting. Thousands of decoys have been painted with sash brush and house paints—the way most baymen did it, and these decoys have probably accounted for more dead birds than all the more modern and carefully painted decoys ever will. That is because there used to be so many more ducks. I suggest that you make a real effort to achieve the more modern and careful painting that the best decoys now have; but if you simply can't do a decent job in that style, you can still adopt the simpler style that will bring in ducks—although not quite as readily.

First we will take up the bayman's style of painting, and with the help of our series of illustrations I will indicate the colors that go on the various areas of the different species, with information on how to mix the colors.

Starting with the black duck: the body color is a brownish black made by mixing black with burnt umber until a dusky color—like burnt cork—is obtained. Flat paints are an absolute requirement, and in thinning them turpentine should be used but not linseed oil. Use only "outside" paints, except for such small details as the wing speculums; these bright colors can be artist's colors which come in small tubes. These may be used with house paint in mixing certain colors. Many old time decoy makers believed that leaving freshly painted stool outdoors at night to become covered with dew tended to reduce the shine of the paint. I think it helps. The finished decoy must be as lacking in shine as possible. The base color for the black duck head is made by mixing a trifle of yellow ochre with some white and burnt umber. The safest plan is to start adding the light colors a bit at a time until the umber has been reduced to a sort of tannish putty color. Some black duck heads are grayish, others more yellowish. In my rig there are several shades of base color on the heads. The feather markings are burnt umber with some black—but not pure black by any means. The body color is right for the head feathering. There are two ways of feathering out the black duck heads. 1) Paint the head the same color as the body. When this is dry put on a coat of the putty color, quite thick in substance so that it won't run, and then with a nail or other sharp instrument, scratch off little lines of the putty color, allowing the dark under coat to show through. This is an easier method for those who aren't accustomed to using fine brushes than 2), which involves painting the putty color on and letting it dry. Then with a fine sable artist's brush painting little lines of burnt umber mixed with black all over the head, with the heavier concentration of streaks that run over each eye and over the top of the head and down the back of the neck. A purple wing speculum can be added as indicated in the illustrations, but it is not really necessary on a decoy painted à la bayman. As noted elsewhere, solid cork black duck bodies are not painted but burnt with a blow torch. Wood and pressed cork must both be painted, the latter with sienna, a trifle of purple and some white; don't make this too light. The back is a medium gray and the sides a lighter shade of gray. Before these two colors have dried run a line of burnt sienna between them and blend it into the upper one as evenly as you can with a dry brush. The under part of the tail is black, and the tail feathers show as a rim of white around the edges of the top of the tail. The speculum is purple bordered at either side by a stripe of white. The ends of the wing feathers on the after end of the back can be indicated with some burnt sienna, and there is a patch of white just forward of the black patch under the tail. The bill is greenish yellow made by mixing a little white and a trace of blue with yellow. The nail is black.

The female mallard's body color is mixed by adding a little burnt sienna to white; then add a little burnt umber, and then a trace of yellow ochre. The effect you want is a lighter color than a black duck, but still a dullish shade—not bright reddish or yellowish. The speculum is purple with a white stripe on each side. The head is similar to a black duck, but add more yellow ochre. The line of dark feathers over the eye is made with black and burnt umber. The bill is orange (yellow, red, plus a little white), with a smudge of black on the upper ridge. Go easy with the black; put a little on your finger and rub it in a bit while the orange is still half wet. Make the edge of this smudge soft, not sharp. The nail is black.

The male pintail's head is about the same color as the mallard's breast—mix burnt umber, white, and a touch of burnt sienna. The back and sides are gray. The lower sides are very light gray, almost white. Down each side of the head and neck runs a pure white streak which runs into the white breast. The rear end of the under body is light tan, with black beyond it and a white stripe around the end of the tail. The top of the tail feathers are black. The bill is black with a light blue patch on each side. When this much painting has thoroughly dried, sharply paint a few long pointed feathers on the after end of the back in black; when dry add a thin line of white on each side of these feathers. These tertiary feathers of the pintail are very characteristic and well worth bothering with. If there are black ducks or female mallards in your rig, don't bother with she pintails; in fact, I don't think they are worth bothering with anyway, as the males are the birds that will be noticed by the live birds.

The male widgeon has a white head with a black-bordered green streak running from around the eye to the base of the neck. The breast is a lighter shade of maroon than the mallard and the color can be mixed by adding more white to the mallard mixture. The back is brownish gray, made by mixing black, white and a bit of burnt umber. Don't get it too dark or too brown. The side is a lighter shade of the breast color, with a shoulder patch of pure white, followed by a stripe of black, in turn followed by a speculum patch of bright green, ended off with a stripe of black. The under tail is white, with black above. A white stripe can be painted around the edge of the tail. The bill is pale blue, with a black nail. I see no reason for making female widgeon as the males will do the attracting in the rig of stool.

The Canada goose has a black head with a pure white chin patch which runs up almost to the eye. The neck is black and the breast light gray. The back and sides are brownish gray made by adding some burnt umber to black and white. There is a big pure white patch at the after under end of the body, and the top of the tail is outlined in black. Both sexes are the same. The bill is black. The eye is dark brown, by the way.

So much for painting decoys à la bayman. Now let's see what it takes to paint a really fine decoy. First of all you must have an assortment of artist's brushes—some flat ones for the larger surfaces and some pointed sable ones for the feathering and other fine lines. The main body colors have been described, and the greater care that you use in painting these on, the better the job will be. The addition of feather markings can be carried just as far as your patience will permit. It recently took me one whole day, really sticking to the job, to feather out nine wooden black ducks. They looked like a million dollars when I finished, and I think black ducks appreciate million dollar decoys!

First of all, always do the complete body painting first, as the head will make a good hand hold for turning the decoy this way and that as you paint in the detail. When the body is completely dry, tackle the head, and the bill, holding the decoy by the body.

Don't have your paints too thin for most of the work, but those used for feathering must not be too thick or you will never finish the job, as the small brushes you use won't hold much paint. Have the paint so that it flows from the brush without running or spreading beyond the area covered by your brush point. You will appreciate what I mean when you start to paint feathers with a small sable brush!

It is utterly impossible for me to explain minutely all the detail work that must be done on each species; I can only show several methods of feathering used on different birds, and then you must try to obtain a superbly painted specimen of the decoy you wish to paint, or refer to the plates in this book and follow them as a guide. If you are a much better artist than I am you can work from a dead bird; but that really requires unusual skill, which probably could be more profitably employed in painting pictures on canvas rather than counterfeit wildfowl.

Black ducks and all the female shoal water ducks can be feathered with either the relatively easy and cruder markings such as this

or each feather may be outlined like this

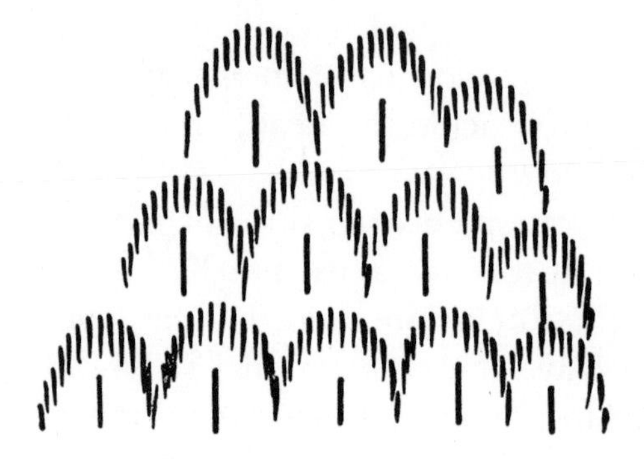

Naturally I don't mean that you should actually paint every feather that may be on a duck, but you can do enough of them to cover the desired areas to give a perfectly lovely effect. And I can assure you that the wild birds appreciate such work, for I have many times seen them drop in with birds so painted, and immediately ruffle their feathers and settle down as peacefully as though I hadn't been within a mile of them. I have also seen birds drop in to crudely painted decoys and take five minutes to settle down; they just knew something wasn't exactly right.

In feathering out a black duck the feathers on the breast are quite small and are indicated by little wavy lines, more or less feather shaped. As you go around the side of the breast, begin to form individual feathers. The feathers on the back are larger, becoming even larger along the sides, and these

Showing head positions from Connett head patterns. Note detail of feather painting.

A duck's-eye view of some of the author's decoys.

Dried paint reticulation on back of broadbill decoy.

The Shang Wheeler black duck. Note beautiful feather painting.

large feathers are carried aft under and to the rear end of the speculum; then they become smaller again around under the tail. The wings, of which the speculums form a part, consist of long overlapping quills that start about halfway down the length of the decoy, on top of the back, separated at the center by about an inch at the forward and end coming to within half an inch of each other at the rear end. Small feathers are shown between the wings. These primary wing feathers end a couple of inches from the tail end of the body, with about half an inch of small feathers between them and the tail feathers, which radiate out to the end of the tail. With some of the thinned out feather paint on your finger smudge light colored overpainting from the forward end of the primaries down to the last four primaries, making the overpainting sharp along the center edges and fading out along the outer sides. This represents the shiny surface of the primaries and gives a very striking appearance of reality. The color used for feathering a black duck is the same as that used on the head, which I have referred to as putty color for want of a better term. It is really a tan shade, rather than a gray putty color. I have told how to mix it. The speculum is deep blue—not too bright—with a black border fore and aft. If you succeed in doing a first class job of feathering, be careful your friend doesn't take a pot shot at the decoy; it will look like a live black duck!

I don't think that this form of feathering can be accomplished on either a solid cork or pressed cork body; it will require the smooth surface of the wooden body to get this fine detail. However, I have done a cruder form of feather painting on my pressed cork decoys and it is very satisfactory. Simply paint thin, rounded lines indicating the curved ends of the feathers, as shown in the first sketch above.

To answer a question that I have been asked: yes, this fine feathering is entirely practical. I first painted my hollow wood black ducks four years ago, and am still using some of them without repainting. Others have had new coats of body color and new feathering, which should be good for another three or four years.

When light fowl—broadbill, canvasback, etc.—are resting in the water, they snuggle down so that their body feathers on the sides come up over the lower edges of the wings to some degree. On the broadbill, for instance, this results in the white side feathers forming a convex curve along the side of the body. Above this curve will be the wings, and then the back is covered with gray feathers reticulated with white. The most beautiful broadbill stool I ever saw sits on my mantelpiece. The reticulation on the back was superbly achieved by a thick layer of heavy, half dry white paint, which finally dried out with little irregular ridges all through it. You may have noticed this effect around the bottom of an old paint can, where the thick paint had dried. Then dark gray paint was wiped over the rough surface, and wiped down so that the raised ridges in the white paint were cleaned off, leaving the gray in the hollows.

A simpler, but very effective way to reticulate is to give the back a coat of white and let it dry. Then put on a coat of gray, using thick paint that will not run. With a comb moving back and forth to make wavy lines as you draw it over the surface of the back, remove the gray to leave the white showing through where the teeth of the comb have passed over it. This makes a beautiful finish. Use a coarse comb.

But the back of a broadbill, male or female, can be reticulated by painting very thin, wavy little lines of white on the back. This same effect can be produced on the back of a canvasback, whose back is really pale gray with white reticulation. In our canvasback painted à la bayman, we simply left the back white. I doubt very much whether it would pay to try to indicate the reticulation on a canvasback. Far more important would be to get the sooty color on the forehead, crown and chin nicely blended around the edges with the rufous color of the head.

To go back to the broadbill again: the head of the lesser scaup is black with a purplish sheen; that of the greater scaup, black with a green sheen. I have found it easier—and perhaps more profitable—to imitate the greenish tinge. It is quite an art to apply the bright green paint to the cheeks and then blend it into the black with a dry brush. You will just have to experiment until you get the knack, and it is well worth getting.

There are two points about doing a good job on the pintail drake that will pay dividends: the correct shape and sweep of the white neck line, and the important tertiary feathers on the after end of the back. The pintail is the most stylish of all wildfowl, and much of this impression is due to the graceful way in which it carries its head, and the way in which its perky tail sits up. It is hardly practical to build the long sharp tail on a decoy. I have seen it done with a metal strip, but heavy usage would soon demolish this. So by correctly painting the after end of the bird we must try to give the stylish impression. This can be heightened greatly by using care in painting the beautiful tertiary feathers, which lay over the end of the wings. The color of these is made by mixing a trifle of yellow ochre with white. These feathers should not be done until the decoy has completely dried, and they must be sharply defined. They run from fore to aft, but those on the outer sides droop downwards. The paint must be thin enough to flow easily from the brush, but not so thin as to run. They are best painted with a sweeping motion, coming to a sharp point at the after end. When this has thoroughly dried, the central feather shafts are painted in a black line down the center of each feather, in such a way that the light color forms a border all around the black quill in the center.

In other words, the black does not extend to the end of the feather, which should show as a long, sharp, light-colored point. Another important feature of the pintail decoy is the lovely speculum, a greenish bronze—or better yet a bronzy green. The forward end of the speculum is light brown, then a broad band of the green, with a little brown overlayed in light, soft streaks—not too many, and carefully! Blend them in. Then a jet black band and behind this a pure white band. I believe in making this speculum quite showy, as it is an important characteristic. The underneath part of the after end of the body is the same buff color that was used for the tertiaries. Aft of this is black, with a pure white streak along each side of the tail. For basic body colors please refer to the earlier description of this (and the other) species.

An old cock widgeon will have a pure white crown on his head; the younger birds have a yellowish tinge to the white. I suggest that the crown be pure white and the cheeks and neck yellowish white, made by adding a trifle of yellow ochre. Always go easy when adding yellow ochre to anything; it is a powerful color, as is burnt sienna; treat them both with respect. Then put the delicate little black feather marks over the cheeks and neck when the head is perfectly dry. The speculum on the widgeon is a brilliant feature, and should be brightly and boldly painted in: first a white shoulder patch several inches long and rounded at the forward end, then a black stripe, followed by a bright green patch, with a black stripe at the after end.

Feathering on a Canada goose is important and easy to accomplish due to the bird's size. The breast is a much lighter brownish gray than the back; some gunners paint the breast white to produce a more showy decoy. In any event it may be quite light. The back color, made with burnt umber, white and black, can be considerably lightened with additional white for the feather markings. These may be rather boldly indicated—not as delicate as duck feathering, as we want them to show; but they must not be startling. Pay a good deal of attention to getting the chin patch of white in just the right position. It starts at the lower after end of the bill and slants upwards and backwards under the eye, rounded off and back to the after end of the chin—where the head meets the neck. This and the pure white under the tail are the two important characteristics of the goose. The primary wing feathers may be indicated at the after end of the body much as those of the black duck were.

The following is a short summary of the colors required for the various species; the methods of mixing them have been covered in this chapter.

Black duck

Body—Flat black, burnt umber
Head—White, yellow ochre, burnt umber
Bill—White, blue, yellow, black, burnt umber
Speculum—Purple, blue, black, white

Mallard drake

Body—Burnt sienna, purple, white, black
Head—Black, green
Bill—White, blue, yellow, black
Speculum—Purple, white

Mallard duck

Body—Burnt sienna, white, burnt umber, yellow ochre
Head—Burnt umber, yellow ochre, white
Bill—Yellow, red, white, black
Speculum—Purple, white

Pintail drake

Body—Black, white, yellow ochre
Head—Burnt umber, white, burnt sienna
Bill—White, blue, black
Speculum—White, burnt umber, green, black

Broadbill drake

Body—White, black
Head—Black, green
Bill—Blue, black, white
Speculum—White

Broadbill duck

Body—Burnt umber, white
Head—Burnt umber, yellow ochre, white
Bill—Blue, black, white
Speculum—White

Canvasback drake

Body—Black, white
Head—Burnt umber, burnt sienna, white, black
Bill—Black
Speculum—None

Canvasback duck

Body—Burnt umber, white, black
Head—Burnt umber, white, yellow ochre
Bill—Black
Speculum—None

Widgeon drake

Body—White, burnt sienna, purple, black, burnt umber
Head—White, black, green, yellow ochre

Bill—Blue, white, black
Speculum—Green, black

Canada Goose

Body—Black, white, burnt umber
Head—Black, white
Bill—Black
Speculum—None

The black, white, burnt umber, yellow ochre, burnt sienna should all be flat house paints. The green, blue, yellow and purple are artist's colors in tubes. Wherever possible, mix the latter colors with some white or other flat house paint; but this is not always possible for brilliant speculum colors.

Before closing this chapter on painting, it might be well to mention that some decoy makers believe in giving the bodies of wooden decoys a good priming coat of lead and oil paint, letting this dry thoroughly, and then painting on the plumage colors. I have never considered this necessary, and I believe that it has certain disadvantages. In use decoys get some pretty rough treatment, and more or less of the paint is rubbed off here and there. I have found that without a priming coat, which, of course, must be a solid color of some kind, there is no paint to show through when the plumage coat is worn down in places, and the bare wood under the plumage coat is sufficiently stained by it to be inconspicuous. Furthermore, I believe that a plumage coat painted directly on the bare wood will be much duller in finish than one applied on top of a priming coat.

CHAPTER X

Ballast Weights, Anchors and Lines

There are two considerations in selecting the ballast weights for your decoys: a shape that will not foul the anchor lines, and the amount of weight required to properly ballast the decoys.

Weights have consisted of strips of lead, links of chain and molded keels. I believe the latter are by far the most satisfactory. The molded weight is flat on top, with a screw cast into the lead so that the weight may be screwed into the keel of the decoy. The lower contour is rounded so that nothing can get caught on it. The absence of sharp edges is desirable from another point of view: when decoys are stacked together there is less chance of a good paint job being injured.

Strips of lead, attached to the keel with copper nails, have been used on thousands of decoys, and, lacking molded weights, are satisfactory. I believe, however, that the molded ballast permits the weight of the lead to exert a greater righting force as it is somewhat lower and more concentrated than the flat strip of lead along the keel of the decoy. Small lead strips do have a very important function when used in conjunction with molded ballast, because very few hand made decoys ride exactly upright in the water, due to such things as heads turned to the side or minor irregularities in body making. I always place a finished decoy in the water and if it requires any trimming ballast, tack a small piece of lead in such a position that it will make the decoy ride perfectly level.

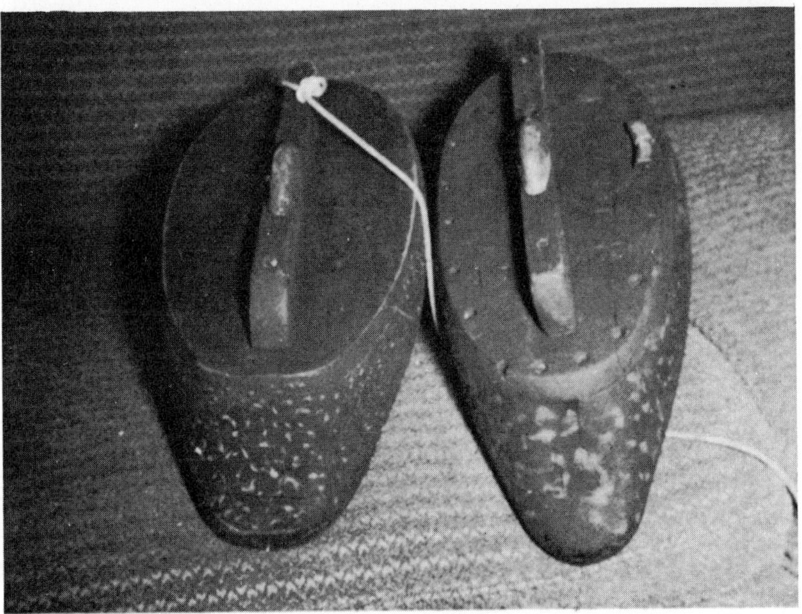

Showing keels, ballast weights, and a small balancing weight.

J. S. Dixon—Fish & Wildlife Service

Peaceful canvasbacks.

J. S. Dixon—Fish & Wildlife Service

Stylish pintails.

In placing the ballast on the keel, bear in mind that the pull of the anchor line on the forward end of the decoy, tends to sink the breast somewhat. This only becomes serious when the bill of the decoy begins to ice up. I have seen a decoy almost disappear in a tideway when iced up. So place the ballast a little further aft than you might normally consider necessary. As each hand made decoy will vary in some degree from its fellows, make the ballasting an individual job.

I have bought molded decoy weights from L.L. Bean of Freeport, Maine, for many years; I have no doubt that they can be had from most manufacturers of decoys. These weights have proved to be just heavy enough for their purpose, and those with brass screws have outlasted those with galvanized screws—which some of the weights were furnished with. However, as I have been using many of these weights for about fifteen years, shifting some of them from one decoy to another, you needn't worry too much about whether they will last satisfactorily. It would not be a big job to cast your own ballast, if you could make or have made the proper mold.

While some of my friends use chain for ballast, I definitely do not like it. As I have pointed out elsewhere, lines tend to foul in the chain, and on a calm day when the decoys move in a gentle sea, the chain can make a most annoying noise which *may* not bother the ducks but does bother me. Furthermore, when a decoy lies on its side, the chain does not exert the straight down pull that firmly placed lead ballast on a keel will exert.

I want to emphasize the necessity for having a decoy perfectly balanced so that it will swim exactly upright. In a heavy sea, with the stool tossing around in various directions, it takes very little to turn an unbalanced decoy over; but a balanced one will soon right itself. Which brings to mind a point that might have been mentioned in the chapter on painting: namely, paint the bottom of your decoys in a color that will not startle ducks if a decoy is upside down. Obviously, the bottom of a black duck should be the regular body color, and a mallard should probably be a neutral gray; broadbill and canvasback should be white. Many gunners put a patch of brilliant red or green or blue on the bottom of their decoys to identify them when picking up from a combined rig, or when a decoy goes adrift and is picked up later. I have a small branding iron with which I burn my name on the bottom of each decoy. One's initials would be equally satisfactory. Oars, bottom boards, backrests and all other wooden equipment in the gunning rig should carry the owner's identification, because I have seen the days when gales have messed things up badly, and some sorting had to be done when the show was over. It also prevents "borrowing."

Should you mount three decoys on an iron rod, as described in Chapter II, there will be no need for ballast—or keels. I might add that decoys may be mounted on rods in pairs.

Many years of experience with various types of decoy anchors have satisfied me that none is the equal of the mushroom anchor. The harder it blows, the stronger the tide runs, the deeper does the mushroom dig into the bottom. The Bellport style of mushroom, properly made, combines every advantage that any other style can boast. First of all it holds; second, it is easy to make; third, it will fit over the head of a decoy after the line has been wound around the body; fourth, it doesn't have to be as heavy as many other types because it depends on its design as well as its weight for its holding properties.

The best way to describe the anchor is to tell you how to make it. First collect a supply of old lead—pipe, or in any other form. Then get a small iron ladle, such as plumbers use, place it on top of a blow torch and put enough lead in the ladle so that when it has melted it will measure about 2½″ across the surface. Meanwhile you will have bent a length of ⅛″ copper, brass or galvanized wire into a circle about 3½″ in diameter. Bend each end of the wire for about ½″ so that you have made two feet for the circle to stand upright on. In shape it will resemble the Greek letter Ω. Slip a ¾″ brass or galvanized ring on the wire. With a pair of pliers grasp the wire circle near the top and hold the feet down in the molten

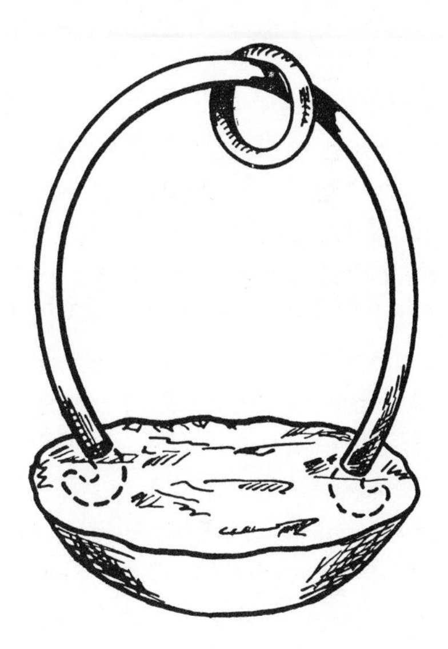

lead until the latter has hardened. You then will have a mushroom anchor, with a ring to which the anchor line is attached. The measurements given are for duck decoys; goose decoys would be made correspondingly larger and heavier, depending on the style and size of the decoy.

If you use copper wire for the shank of the anchor, be sure not to use a galvanized ring on it, because salt water will start electrolysis and soon ruin the ring. Brass rings are satisfactory when used on copper or brass shanks; galvanized rings for galvanized shanks.

Another style of mushroom anchor is made by inserting in the molten lead a piece of heavy copper wire which has been bent double and the ends turned out at right angles. When the lead has hardened, open the top of the bent wire, to form a loop about half an inch in diameter, by inserting any suitable tool; then twist the wire upon itself to form a twisted shank with a loop for the anchor line at the top. It is better to have a small ring in this loop to which the line may be attached, because there is heavy wear on the line at this point, as well as at the point of attachment on the decoy. This style of mushroom holds very well, but lacks the feature of fitting over the decoy head.

When you see one of your decoys start to drift off down wind at a good rate of speed, you can be sure that the anchor line has let go, and you may be equally sure that it has let go where it is attached to either the anchor or the decoy. There are two satisfactory knots for anchor lines. The first, which I use, is the bowline; I have never had one let go. The second is tied by pushing a loop of the line, after a figure eight knot has been tied in its end, through the tie ring on the anchor. Then bring the knotted end of the line around and through the loop. Pull the loop up tight, and you have a knot with a double thickness of line taking the strain where it passed through the ring. This knot is much more satisfactory when used directly through the wire loop of a twisted shank mushroom, than when used with a tie ring. I recommend the bowline, both at the anchor and at the decoy, but always pass the line through the ring *twice* before tying the knot.

More lines give way at the decoy than at the anchor in my experience. When a keel is used, a hole is bored through it within an inch or so from its forward end, and the edges of this hole must be rounded and smooth to prevent chafe. Use a counter sink, then a rat tail file, and then sandpaper to make this hole smooth and easy. Pass the line through it twice, and then tie a bowline. If a rawhide loop is used follow the same procedure: twice through the loop, and a bowline. Every season, if my lines are still in good condition, I untie the bowlines, snip a few inches off the end of the lines, and retie; this removes the part of the line that carries the biggest strain and where chafe occurs.

Remember: it's always in a heavy blow that decoys break loose, and that is not the most convenient time to have to chase them. Every so often during the season inspect all your lines; replace any which look chafed or weak, and avoid the loss of anchors which occurs when a stool drifts away. I never use a line for more than two years, no matter how nice it may look. I have learned the hard way that it doesn't pay.

For years I used heavy, tarred cod line for anchor lines. Then a friend presented me with a hank of 1/8″ braided line, dyed olive drab color. I haven't been able to find out exactly what this line is or where it came from; but it is the best I have ever had—better than the tougher looking cod line, strangely enough. The latter seems to chafe easier. I believe this cotton line is known as braided yacht signal line. Nylon should make a first class anchor line, if you are feeling rich. I presume that it could be dyed a neutral shade, as *white line must never be used on decoys;* in clear water it shows up badly, and ducks don't like it.

Several years ago I was lying in my punty on the point of a small island. Directly to windward of me was a deep cove with a skim of ice about half an inch thick covering most of it. Later in the day about an acre of this ice let go and started to drift down on my rig. Being a bit of an optimist I watched it approach, and tried to believe that the wind would take it clear of my stool. When it had almost reached my rig I suddenly discovered that it wasn't going to drift clear, and something had to be done mighty fast if I weren't to lose my decoys. The only thing to do was jump overboard with my shoving oar—about nine feet long—and begin sweeping decoys three and four at a time onto the point, clear of the ice. By the time I was through I was exhausted and you never saw such a mess as my stool. But the point of the tale is that if my lines hadn't been in first class shape, and my decoys in good condition, neither would have stood the terrific strain of being swept out of the ice.

To function properly mushroom anchors must be rigged with long enough lines so that the pull on the anchor will be along the bottom rather than up from it. This means a line about 7 feet long for a depth of water of 2 feet. In other words, the line should be about three times the depth of the water. Don't forget that in a gale water may rise several feet, as well as fall. If very heavy anchors are used, the lines need not be so long; but as weight can be an important consideration in a duck rig, I would rather lug line than lead. Heavy, over-size decoys will require more weight and longer lines than smaller stool. I belabor this point of anchoring decoys so that they will stay put under all conditions, because I have seen rigs carried away, or odd stool break loose so many, many times in my years of gunning.

CHAPTER XI

Setting Out Decoys

Perhaps a few hints on setting out the beautiful decoys you have made may help you get better results from them.

Every point or location will have its separate problem, largely depending on the direction of the wind. And there is quite a difference in the way you rig for shoal water ducks and divers.

First of all, shoal water ducks do not like to fly directly at the land, particularly if they have been gunned. It is much wiser to give them open water to approach the stool over, and open water ahead of the stool, so that they can avoid flying over the land. Normally, shoal water ducks will come up to the tail of the stool, fly along over or just outside and drop in at the head. Right handed gunners who don't like to shoot to the right, can usually rig their decoys and place themselves so that they can get a shot off to the left. For instance: If the wind is blowing from your left, set out your decoys so that you will be sitting near the tail of the rig; the birds will probably lead from your right to your left to the head of the stool, and you will be able to get your shot toward your left, if you let the birds go until they are near the head of the rig.

If the wind is blowing from your right, the birds will come from your left and swing up along the stool. If you place yourself at the head of the stool you will be able to take your shot a bit to your left as the birds come in over the decoys. If you are carefully hidden and don't move a finger as birds come

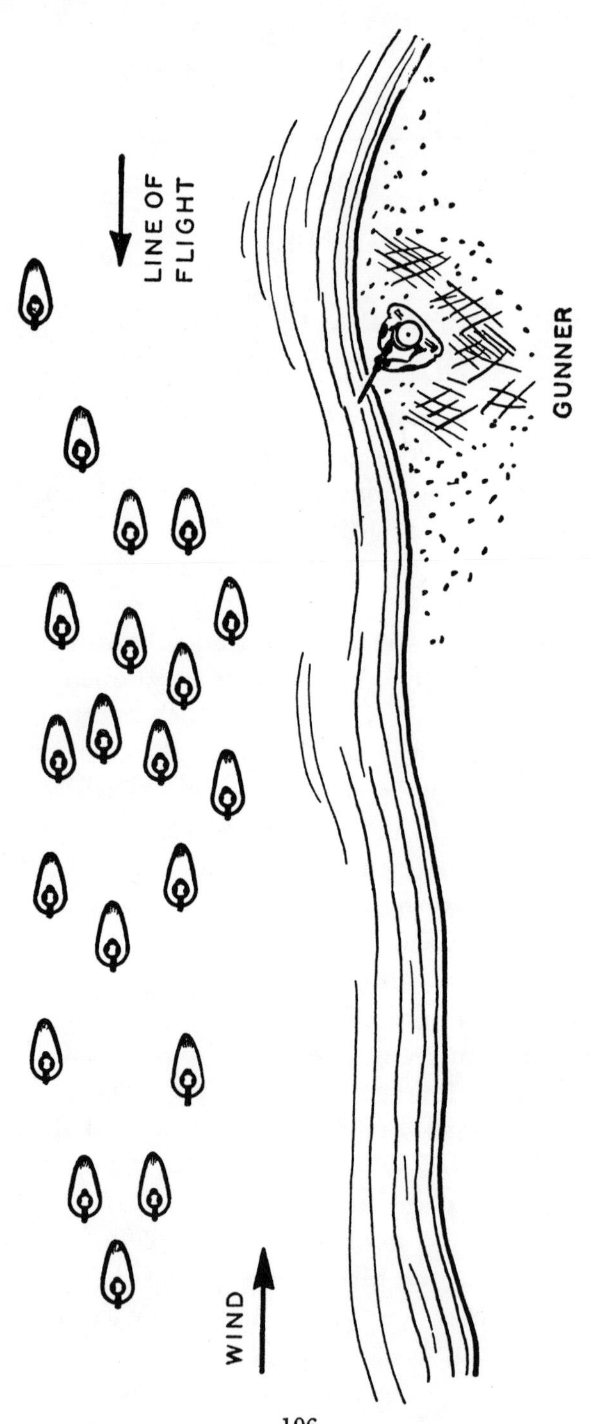
LINE OF
FLIGHT
GUNNER
WIND

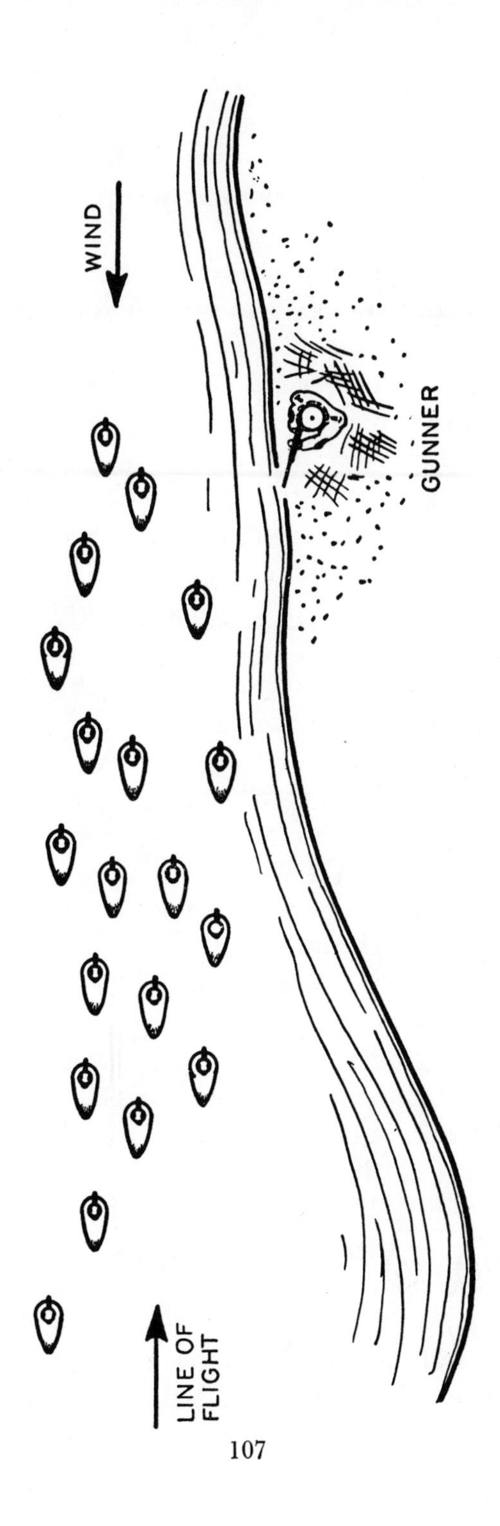
WIND
GUNNER
LINE OF
FLIGHT

in, and you use good decoys, you can make birds lead just about as you want them by the way you place the decoys and yourself in relation to them.

The usual way to set out decoys for shoal water ducks is in an irregular string about 10 to 20 feet wide and as long as your supply of decoys will permit. Set them fairly thick at the tail of the rig, with several decoys trailing off to leeward. Up near the head of the rig leave an open space, as an invitation to drop in there. Put one or two leaders out ahead. If birds are swinging up too far outside of the rig, move three or four tail stool out in a crescent, extending maybe as much as fifteen yards. Birds will often pick up those wide birds and then swing along the line of decoys instead of flying too far outside of them.

Sometimes you can rig your stool in two halves with a path about 10 feet wide down the center of the rig, in order to tempt the birds to drop into this open path. Place a few tip ups in the tail end of the path. I don't mean that you should entice the birds to land in your decoys so that you can shoot them on the water, but I do mean that you want to make them *want* to land in it and then shoot before they do.

Diving ducks are inclined to fly over a rig of decoys and land inside—something shoal water birds almost never are tempted to do. You should therefore set light fowl stool further out from your position, with a few decoys at the head of the rig leading in toward the shore. The birds will then probably cross over the rig and want to drop in with the decoys on the inshore side of it. This same plan may be used for shoal water birds by stringing the main rig closer to shore with a group at the head running offshore. The birds would then be tempted to drop in ahead of or behind these offshore birds.

If you have half a dozen pintail and widgeon decoys with your rig of black ducks and mallards, put them somewhere

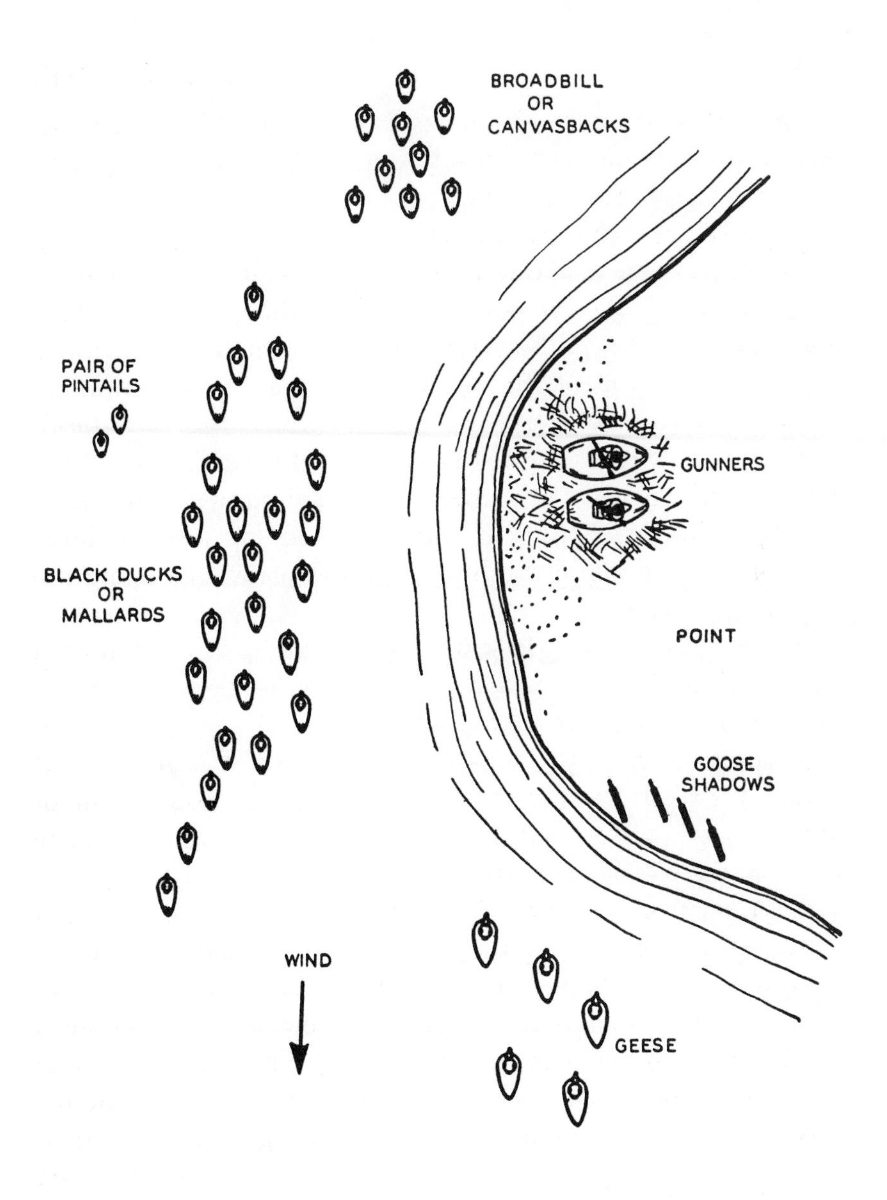
BROADBILL
OR
CANVASBACKS
PAIR OF
PINTAILS
GUNNERS
BLACK DUCKS
OR
MALLARDS
POINT
GOOSE
SHADOWS
WIND
GEESE

in the rig all bunched together, so that they will show up better than if they were scattered through the rig. Either at the head or about the middle of the rig will probably be better than at the tail, where some good big oversize tollers will do more good. If you are going to rig a set of divers and a set of shoal water decoys together, put the former well inside the latter, and a bit to windward of them. Diving ducks don't seem to have any objection to flying over dippers, but the reverse is not true.

In very rough weather you can set out your decoys closer to your blind than you can in calm water. Bunch them quite close together so that they show up in rough water; spread them out generously and they will show up better when things are smooth.

Never hesitate to shift your rig if conditions seem to call for it. Sometimes I have started birds coming to me by merely shifting half a dozen out of thirty decoys. Sometimes the whole rig has to be moved, especially if the wind shifts; don't sit looking at it and putting off the job; get it done as soon as you are sure what should be done, and then hope your change will bring birds in. It drives me crazy to lie to a rig that I know isn't right; it takes all the fun out of the thing. It's better to make a change of some kind than stewing about it, as you probably won't shoot very well in a stew. And the satisfaction of rigging so that birds come in like chickens on a wire, is even greater than killing a few that don't like anything about your rig. With only four birds to be shot in one whole day, you will have plenty of time to experiment—although I will have to confess that every time you wade out into your stool, that is just the time when you will see birds in the air! Having made your decoys, learn to use them to the best possible advantage.

And now a final and extremely important word: no matter how beautiful your decoys may be, and no matter how skillfully you may have rigged them out, all will be wasted if you don't remain ABSOLUTELY STILL when birds are coming in or flying around near you. I can count on the fingers of one hand the men I have shot with who don't grab for their guns or turn their heads for a better view of the birds when you whisper "Don't Move! Coming from the right!" It is, of course, important that you be well hidden in your boat or blind; but it is infinitely more important that you keep perfectly still in the presence of birds. I'd rather lie right out in the open and keep absolutely motionless than to have a good hide and move.

Several years ago I was shooting with a young friend and a guide on the Chesapeake. We were in a stake blind—the kind that is built several hundred yards from the shore and big enough to hold three or four men, with a space under it for the boat. The sun was shining in such a way that if we moved in the blind, a shadow was cast on the back wall of it. But I didn't discover this until three or four birds had swerved out of gunshot as they approached the rig. Then I noticed that on the approach of birds my friend and I would shift along the inside of the blind, well below the front of it, in order to take the best position from which to shoot. Although we couldn't be seen by birds out in front, our shadows certainly could, and we lost quite a few shots before we learned to hold perfectly still.

There just isn't any situation in which you can afford to move when birds are coming toward your rig, and unless you are willing to stay motionless, don't waste your time making a set of beautiful decoys.

Index